The Half-Shut Eye

The Half-Shut Eye

Television and Politics in Britain and America

JOHN WHALE

GREENWOOD PRESS, PUBLISHERS
WESTPORT, CONNECTICUT

Library of Congress Cataloging in Publication Data

Whale, John, 1931-
    The half-shut eye.

    Reprint. Originally published: London : Mac-
millan ; New York : St. Martin's Press, 1969.
    Includes bibliographical references and index.
    1. Television in politics--Great Britain.
2. Television in politics--United States. I. Title.
[HE8700.7.P6W5 1981]   320   81-4108
ISBN 0-313-23036-6 (lib. bdg.)   AACR2

First published 1969 by Macmillan & Co. Ltd.

Reprinted with the permission of The Macmillan Press Ltd.

Reprinted in 1981 by Greenwood Press
A division of Congressional Information Service, Inc.
88 Post Road West, Westport, Connecticut 06881

Printed in the United States of America

10 9 8 7 6 5 4 3 2 1

Acknowledgments

My thanks are due to Independent Television News, my employers for nine years, who gave me opportunity both to accumulate the elements for this book and to write it; and also to those friends on both sides of the Atlantic who read the typescript and suggested improvements.

Washington, November 1968

To J. S. W.

Contents

PART I

Introduction

1 The Limits of Vision

The memorial film to Senator Robert Kennedy had ended some fifteen minutes before. Several hundred of the delegates to the 1968 Democratic national convention were still on their feet, beating time as they sang 'Glory, glory, hallelujah, His truth goes marching on'. Suddenly a small, stout figure got up from his seat. He pointed to a henchman on the speakers' rostrum just in front of him. The signal was retransmitted; and at once a wide section of the public gallery broke out in counter-cheers and freshly printed signs which read 'We love Mayor Daley'. The king of the host city of Chicago had decided to reassert his control.

Richard Daley felt no need for concealment. In the amphitheatre his security men could be seen arranging a loyal response to the speech in which Hubert Humphrey would soon accept the party's presidential nomination. Outside the convention hotels on Michigan Avenue the Illinois National Guard, the Mayor's guests, were discouraging any show of disagreement with the party's Vietnam policies. The Mayor had already said he found nothing more than over-reaction in the way the same disagreement had been met the night before by the Chicago police.

All this was faithfully shown on television in many countries. In the United States much of it was shown at the moment it happened.

Yet television viewers did not see quite all they needed to see. Television had to contend with certain limitations, some imposed and some inherent, in recounting what happened during those four days in late August.

The most obvious and least important limitations were physical. One Columbia Broadcasting System reporter was knocked down by security men, and another taken into custody, on the convention floor itself. More than other journalists, television cameramen and their equipment were assailed by the forces of order in the streets. This hostility arose from the belief in many conformist minds that nonconformist behaviour is encouraged when it is reported on television: a belief which broadcasters themselves knew to have some validity, and felt obliged to take account of.

Slightly more sophisticated obstacles were also put in television's way. In the amphitheatre, camera teams were not allowed enough tickets to get them onto the convention floor. Away from it there was another problem. A strike by men who were to help install television equipment had been temporarily settled, after Mr Daley had intervened, on terms which confined live coverage to the amphitheatre itself. But the crucial part of the convention, the attempt by candidates and a whole coalition of dissidents to change Mr Humphrey's mind about the usefulness of the Vietnam war or to deny him the nomination, would largely take place at the convention hotels and in front of them. The American networks decided to cover what happened there from videotape vans and send the videotape by motor-cycle to the amphitheatre for transmission. The city authorities were not defeated. They decreed that the vans could not be parked in front of the hotels: they would be confined in car parks at the back.

When the networks made head against these difficulties and gave ocular proof of Chicago police habits, the Mayor cried foul: not enough had been done to show that the dissidents in the streets were terrorists who had vowed to paralyse the city. Yet the proof was clear, in the Mayor's view: 'they had maps locating the hotels and routes of buses for the guidance of terrorists from out of town'. For the best part of half an hour of live evening television Mr Daley was allowed to offer evidence of this quality to the chief CBS anchorman with scarcely an objection interposed. The interview did not result from corporate prudence, although it appeared to. It was an effort after even-handedness by a journalist who knew how vulnerable broadcasting organisations are when they can be made to seem unfair in their dealings with authority.

These were some of the external influences on television that week. More serious were the innate handicaps. Television viewers were never given more than a cursory explanation of why the mayor of a provincial city was able to rule not merely his own region but a national political convention with an iron fist. They could not have been: the structure of patronage was too complex, too abstract, too private to be set out on television. There was nothing to photograph. Again, television reporters passed on a great deal of opinion and conjecture about the plans of Senator Edward Kennedy, who sat out the entire convention on Cape Cod. But the cameras could get no nearer the actual processes of decision which led to the Senator's lingering denials of interest in the nomination than the front door of the Chicago club where his brother-in-law Stephen Smith was holding court.

Television cameras in the amphitheatre showed President Johnson's local lieutenant sitting on the rostrum behind the bank of switches that worked the microphones on the convention floor. They could not show to what extent the president still controlled from Texas the gathering he had planned as a Texas-sized sixtieth-birthday party for himself; nor to what extent the Daley security arrangements, the ushers in frogged uniforms and the magnetised plastic cards which delegates had to wear round their necks, were still in accord with the original Johnson scheme.

The emphasis of television's coverage, in short, was unavoidably graphic rather than analytical. Pictures were rightly held more precious than words. But where pictures could not tell the story, there were gaps in the telling.

Where they could tell it, of course, they were unrivalled. Some of the most effective television comments on the Chicago convention were made without spoken words at all. During the closing credits of the National Broadcasting Company's *Today* show, the morning after the convention had ended, a cheerful male voice sang a song of which the tune had been much played during the week, often in Mr Daley's honour: 'My kind of town, Chicago is'. On the screen, half-hidden under the names of producers and film editors, as if it were too everyday a part of Chicago life even to be worth a good look, a trio of Chicago policemen could be seen about their work: helmeted, shirtsleeved, their billy-clubs busy in their hands, they bundled young men and girls one at a time into a Black Maria. 'My kind of razzmatazz...'

The purpose of the whole security panoply was to make Chicago safe for Mr Humphrey's nomination. That purpose was duly achieved. The fact that television's testimony about the methods used had so little effect on the outcome is not necessarily something to deplore; though the whole question of the very patchy influence of television on the choice of political leaders has to be examined. But those four days in Chicago did illustrate some of the real weaknesses of television in reporting political news. Television was shown to be still comparatively easily hampered by physical obstacles: to be sensitive to the charge of intensifying the action it reported by the mere act of reporting it: to be hobbled by its delicate and yet unbreakable links with authority: to be powerless to reach the moment as distinct from the outward sign of political decision; and to be wedded for better or worse to pictures.

It has sometimes been maintained that the chief obstacles to properly informative reporting on television are commercial. There is undoubtedly a case here. It has been documented by the man whom President Kennedy appointed chairman of the Federal Communications Commission.[1]* A president of the CBS news division resigned his job on the same score and wrote a book about it.[2] The charge arises in America because most broadcast programmes are financed directly by advertisers. In principle the sponsor has no say in what goes on the air. In practice he has a simple sanction: if he dislikes the programme he need not pay for it any more. If he objects to the way a news programme chooses or handles the news, he can put his money into something else.

In this as in other matters, it is helpful to set American practice side by side with British. Although advertisers on Independent Television in Britain simply buy time in between programmes which are entirely devised by the broadcasting company, ITV news programmes look remarkably like American ones. So do news programmes on the British Broadcasting Corporation's channels, which at present carry no advertising. It is true that ITV still has to draw an audience, to keep its advertising rates up; and so does the BBC, if it is to be allowed an occasional increase in the licence fee demanded of all viewers which finances it. Yet in America, where more and more private money goes into non-commercial broadcasting, there are news broadcasters freed even from the obligation to be popular. Starting in November 1967, the Public Broadcast Laboratory had twelve million dollars from the Ford Foundation to spend in two seasons of weekly programmes about current events. Sunday after Sunday it turned out to be doing, rather more clumsily, what the commercial networks had been doing for years.

The curbs on television's coverage of news and politics are more subtle and extensive than can be explained simply in terms of human greed.

*

[1]*All notes are at the back of the book. They contain nothing except references to published work.

The profession of politics is traditionally a watchful one. Pope, in *The Rape of the Lock*, pretended that the politician had the ability to 'see through all things with his half-shut eyes'.[3] Politicians are still believed to be on constant if sometimes drowsy watch for their rivals, or their opponents, or the main chance. But it is a condition of democracy that politicians and people in government should themselves be watched, so that their performance can be checked and stimulated. Television has become for most voters in Britain and America the chief supplier of this service: the electorate's eye on politics and politicians. Yet the round, unwinking gaze of the television camera is not as all-vigilant as it may seem. Natural and artificial causes conspire to ensure that its eye too, like the politician's in Pope, is no more than half open.

PART II

Television and Events

2 Picture-Dealers

Television is pictures. It feeds on them. It must always have them. There can be silence on the screen: no words, no music, no sound effects: but there must be pictures. This is the first datum that all television journalists have to come to terms with.

They are not much beset by any sense that as many pairs of eyes as possible must watch what they do. Other people in the organisation take care of that. They are there to offer an account or an explanation of what the course of events has put in front of them. They are not in search of viewers; but they are in search of viewability. In their approach to any happening they must consider first where the pictures are.

This is no problem if the happening is a train crash near Dijon or a fireworks show in Luxembourg, except in so far as distance creates difficulties. Nor need it be a problem if the story is about poverty in Mississippi. Although poverty is an idea, pictures can make it a less abstract one.

But not all ideas are so simply pictorial. In April 1967 a subcommittee of the United States Senate made an unsuccessful attempt to ward off danger in the following year through a reform of the system whereby the making of the president rested not with the electorate but with an electoral college, voting by states according to the popular majority in each; and failing them, with the House of Representatives. The system could produce confusion and worse. In the nineteenth century it had three times come up with a president who had won fewer votes from the people than his opponent.

The problem seemed worth setting out for British viewers; and an idea that was manageable on paper became at once intractable. There were no pictures.

The only pictures of the event, if they had been available, would have shown party workers who had been rewarded with college membership gathering on the appointed day more than two years before in fifty state capitols and elsewhere. They were not available, and they would have been very dull if they had been. In the end the best source of pictures that came to hand in Washington was the licence plates of cars. They had the names of different states on, sometimes with slogans or even pictures; and they moved, and they could be photographed in appropriate settings. But as a guide to an eighteenth-century constitutional compromise they left some things unexplained.

In August 1966, to take another instance, the idea first became current in London that President de Gaulle of France was waging a deliberate 'gold battle' against Britain and America: the battle which became fiercer after the British devaluation of November 1967 and resulted in an end to the gold pool and to total dollar convertibility in March 1968. As a form of protest against increasing direct investment by American private industry in France, and against Anglo-Saxon attitudes in general, the Bank of France had for some time been sending its resulting surplus of dollars back to the United States and cashing them in for American gold; as the rules of the gold exchange standard then provided. Independent Television News, the news division of ITV, sent me to Paris from London to piece together some film of all this. The assignment disclosed some of the barriers television comes up against in reporting the overseas economic movements which are the governing factors in Britain's domestic political life.

Jacques Rueff, the man who taught President de Gaulle to abominate the gold exchange standard, gave us an interview on the terrace of his eighteenth-century manor house in Normandy. The view stretched to the huge Tancarville suspension bridge across the lower Seine. M. Rueff had a small bar-billiards table just inside the house, and he was happy to hit a few balls about on it for us, although his wife thought it gave a wrong impression. The pictures were good. The talk was less good, and for cause. Mme Rueff saw to it that we worked fast: the sun was high, her husband was virtually bald, and the cameraman could not allow him to wear a hat because the top half of his face would have come out black. Worse, the English that he had learnt as a financial counsellor in the French Embassy in London over thirty years before had fallen into disuse. The charm and precision of his native speech were destroyed in a foreign tongue. His clinching point about the advantages to businessmen of a return to the gold standard was wrecked because he translated 'bénéfice' as benefit instead of profit.

We still had to find pictures to illustrate gold flow. The best we got were of dealing on the Paris stock exchange. It had very little to do with the matter in hand: the gold and currency exchanges were down below in the cellar. But they were very staid affairs; whereas the trading in stocks produced a good volume of sound – the Bourse can be heard several streets away – and the screen was filled with men in rimless glasses waving and shouting without taking their cigarettes out of their mouths. But even this small success was counterproductive: when the film was put together these pictures were quite good enough to distract attention from the script's attempt at explaining about French companies with American money in them.

Unsurprisingly, we were not allowed into the Bank of France to film their gold. All we could do was to show the extent of the building by driving up and down outside and filming barred windows; and the gilt statue of Joan of Arc in the rue de Rivoli had to serve as a sign of the mystic appeal of gold to the French heart. The resulting programme ran for twenty-five minutes. A newspaper piece covering the same ground could have been read in five and would have left a clearer impression.

American television reporters found all these difficulties written infinitely larger in a real battlefield: Vietnam. Some of them called it the first television war. Within the limits set by the American commanders in the field, by the cumbrousness of film gear and by common prudence, television news teams got the pictures. The achievement represented a huge advance in the coverage of war. Its realities were inescapably presented: South Vietnamese village people weeping for their burnt homes, the bodies of dead Viet Cong picked up in a helicopter net and bulldozed into a hole in the ground, a dying American soldier taking what comfort he could from an army chaplain beside a path through a rice-field. These pictures left people all over the world with much less excuse than they had before for not being able to understand or imagine what war is. They were almost enough to foster the hope that as a method of settling disputes war might go out of fashion; except that there had been no such result from comparable advances in war reporting in the past – William Howard Russell for *The Times* in the Crimea, or radio correspondents in the Second World War. Indeed, some sociologists maintained that the savage scenes on television simply made violence a more customary part of western life.

Helpful or not, the work of American television crews only covered one side of the war. They knew this themselves. The other side went largely unreported on television: the struggle to give the people of South Vietnam an atmosphere of security they could live in, an economy they could work in and a government they could believe in. Television reporters found, as American officials did, that these problems were too nebulous, progress in them too difficult of measurement; and chiefly that there were no pictures. If the battlefield was indeed the hearts and minds of men, as the phrase ran, then no film could be brought back from it. The best that could be had were the commonplaces of all social-action films: rows of pacification workers doing exercises in white shirts, close-up of white hand tipping rice ration into bowl held by brown hand, back view of schoolchildren looking at a blackboard. And if a television journalist decided to grapple with these difficulties and compile a story none the less, his film might be shelved when it got back to New York in favour of a search-and-destroy mission in the Mekong Delta or streetfighting in Hue. Of the two wars, Americans saw much less of the one they stood in much more need of winning.

It is true that even if the pictures in television news coverage are sometimes inadequate, the words are there in support. The voice of the journalist in the studio or in the field can add to the pictures and explain them and give them a meaning which they may not inherently have; so that television news still exists in two dimensions where all other methods of reporting have for the most part only one.

But the broadcast word has a limitation. It cannot be called back. If a man is reading a newspaper story about public comment on a government proposal to change the basis of unemployment insurance in Britain, and cannot remember the details of the existing system, he can run his eye back up the column and look for a reminder. But if he is watching a television programme, or for that matter listening to a radio broadcast, he cannot ask for a replay of an earlier passage. On the rare occasions when he is granted a replay, as viewers of football programmes sometimes are, it is at someone else's direction.

As a rule he has no second chance. Gaps in his knowledge or understanding stay unfilled. So broadcasters work under the obligation of being immediately understood, with no going back; and before an audience of greatly varying education and intelligence.

For this reason the broadcaster has to be careful all the time that what he says should be simple; and for the television broadcaster it has to be picturable as well.

This is the equipment that television brings to the reporting of politics. Politicians already have an urge to simplify: partly to be understood, partly to be persuasive, partly because they may not fully understand the issue themselves. Television abets them.

One of the classic simplifications in British politics was the argument about nuclear defence. During the general election of October 1964 the Labour party, as the opposition seeking power, campaigned on a manifesto which described the independent British deterrent promised by the Conservatives after the Nassau agreement as a 'nuclear pretence'. It would not be British, the Labour manifesto said, and it would not be independent, and it would not deter. All three negatives were much too categoric to fit the facts. Leading Conservative speakers went all the other way. Sir Alec Douglas-Home, in his last days as Conservative Prime Minister, constantly spoke as if the Polaris submarines which were to constitute the new force were already patrolling the seas with their lethal load complete and their admiral looking to nowhere but Downing Street for orders, unless perhaps it was Buckingham Palace. One of the most vivid pictures of that election which comes to mind is of Sir Alec, dressed in beautiful tweeds, standing in the setting sun on a hay-cart at the foot of a sloping meadow in Suffolk, and telling a loyal gathering that a Conservative government would never give away the deterrent. He would never take the decision about the future of Britain out of the hands of the Queen's ministers and the Queen's parliament. The whole scene was admirable television: the pictures were good, the words were plain; and the impression left with the voter was as distant from the real complexities of the situation as the arguments used on the other side. Four years later, under a Labour government, Polaris missiles had been test-fired from a British submarine off the coast of Florida and the British Polaris programme was still grinding slowly towards completion.

Of course television can deal in difficult ideas, just as politicians can. Both sometimes attempt it. If there are no pictures, the camera simply shows the picture of the man who is expounding the idea or offering the information.

This seems obvious enough. Some of television's greatest successes have been won in this way, with pictures of people talking. Social scientists have often demonstrated, if it needed demonstrating, that there is nothing so compelling as personal influence.[1] Here is television working its proper work: taking one person's influence to several other people all at once.

There are problems about this. One is that personal influence translated onto television is no longer personal. The same social scientists agree that television, along with other methods of communication in indeterminate order, ranks behind personal influence as a persuader. The lay explanation of this may be that a television picture gives equal prominence to every item in a whole face, or a whole head and shoulders; so that a strand of eyebrow descending in front of an eye, or strongly patterned clothes, or a shiny ornament, can claim very much more of a listener's attention than they would in a face-to-face duologue, when his instinct is to give most of his attention to a speaker's eyes and mouth. Perhaps more influential, the ordinary rules of behaviour shame most people into at least the pretence of more attentiveness to a flesh-and-blood interlocutor than they feel obliged to accord a television set.

But the chief weakness of this kind of presentation is that it is not what television is for. It is a waste of opportunity. It is what Madison Avenue men call 'radio with a light to read by'. The picture adds nothing: indeed, it may subtract, in the sense that it distracts. If the special talent of television is to be properly exploited, the pictures and the words must reinforce each other. The watcher must see what he is hearing about, and hear about what he is seeing. One of the more interesting exercises in television is to write the words that accompany film. The writer may not have been there when the film was shot, and if he was he may not have had much control over what shots were taken or how they were later cut together. He knows how many feet of film there are in each shot, and he knows how many words he may write to each foot. With that equipment he must try to make it appear that every foot of the film was garnered and arranged to illustrate every facet of the truths he is intent on relaying. More circumscribed than sonneteers, scriptwriters in television news have to be contented again and again with twenty feet of film at five words a foot.

But often there is no film. And the conscientious television journalist, shying away from radio with a light to read by, turns next to charts and graphs and diagrams.

They do not always work. The short reason is that if they say the same thing as the broadcaster is saying they irritate, and if they say something different they distract. They can load the viewer with more to understand than he has time for; and since the picture on most people's television sets is less well shaped and defined than the picture on a control-room monitor, they can be difficult to read.

The sad fact is that for many of the ideas in which television coverage of current affairs must trade there are no useful illustrations possible. The vital details of a rent bill are not made clearer by little drawings of houses. Economics defy pictures altogether. For tolerant viewers, the balance of trade can perhaps be illustrated yet again by a picture of crates at the docks; but there is nothing to be done for the balance of payments. After all, it specifically includes what British economists call invisibles.

Television does not simply need pictures. It needs interesting pictures. But people are not disposed to be interested by what they see every day. So there is a premium on the unusual, the abnormal.

Television is often castigated as if it were unique in this. 'We have more than three million young people serving in uniform', President Johnson said to three television interviewers in December 1967 when the talk turned to people who demonstrated their dislike of the Vietnam war. 'They don't get the attention that you television people give these exhibitionists. They are just there from daylight to dark, fighting for freedom and liberty, and willing to die for it.'

In fact it suited President Johnson well to have it represented that everyone who fought the war was doing it out of conscience and everyone who objected was doing it out of exhibitionism; and if some television reporting made this a tenable belief, there were newspaper accounts that kept it company. A group of fourteen eminent academics in the field of political science had implied as much a week before, in a document issued from the Freedom House Public Affairs Institute in New York, when they claimed that 'an unfortunately large portion of the mass media' were concentrating on the most sensationalist and extreme events of the time.

In the minds of the dons and the President may have been the Washington demonstration of two months earlier; when some tens of thousands of people had gathered at the Lincoln Memorial on a shining autumn day, listened to speeches against the Vietnam war, walked across the Potomac to the Pentagon and found themselves confronted by military policemen and civilian marshals. There a detachment of them tried unsuccessfully to storm the building, and slowly dispersed during the evening and night. It was the newspapers just as much as television which under-represented the church-picnic atmosphere of the first part of the day in favour of the scuffles of the second part. Worried middle age had to make way, even in the published reports, for vociferous youth.

Yet perhaps television is under stronger pressures than newspapers to show the abnormal at the expense of the normal. The trouble with the normal is that it is dull: it has been seen before. Most newspapers can afford dull patches, because no one expects to read a newspaper right through. News broadcasts cannot, on television or radio: if they once lose a listener's willing attention he may switch his set off altogether – or worse, switch it to another station.

Again, the sheer brevity of broadcast news programmes leaves little room except for the remarkable. CBS once calculated that the words spoken in their main evening news bulletin, which has to share half an hour with up to five minutes' worth of advertisements, would fill no more than six of the eight columns on the front page of the *New York Times*.

These arguments apply to radio as much as television. But although sounds can be as emotive as pictures, they are nothing like as explicit. They cannot be left to themselves as an account of events for more than a few seconds. So even the most exciting sounds need not pre-empt all the space available for a report of what happened. Nor are sound effects indispensable to radio in the way pictures are to television. A radio reporter can give a good account of events in words alone, without any recourse to the noise of marchers singing or military commands. But a television report can be no better than its pictures. Dull pictures and interesting words will still make a dull story.

Television's special problems in avoiding the appearance of sensationalism were illustrated in the report published in March 1968 by the presidential commission which had been appointed under Governor Otto Kerner of Illinois to enquire into the city riots of the previous summer.[2] Although newspapers, radio and television made a real effort, the commissioners said, to give a balanced and factual account of the disorders, 'the overall effect was, we believe, an exaggeration of both mood and event'. Their chief complaint was that the riots were reported not enough as a rejection of life in the ghetto and too much as a war between black and white; and they seemed to attach the chief blame to television when they said that television newscasts 'tended to emphasise law enforcement activities, thereby overshadowing underlying grievances and tensions'.

Their evidence for this was that although the 955 television sequences their staff examined were predominantly calm in tone, there were a lot of policemen, national guardsmen and soldiers in the pictures. It took a special conference with journalists at Poughkeepsie in November 1967 to point out to the commissioners that television cameramen dwelt on those scenes because that was the best they could get. It was unlikely that a camera crew would be on the scene when trouble first erupted: the most they could do was to arrive in time to see the forces of order trying to manage the situation.

During the four days of the Detroit riots in July 1967, several television units spent some of the hours of daylight photographing the places where Negroes lived. It was the nearest we could come to the despair of the ghetto. But the detail of buildings does not come out well on television, and the pictures were too static to be held for long. During part of each night we drove round the town. Because of the curfew, there was no one to be seen except the press and the forces of order. Although the streets were not lit, we took such pictures as we could to show their emptiness, and to show that this was not a whole city in flames. But it seemed unlikely that these pictures could be interesting to look at for more than thirty seconds. We fell back perforce on the activities of the federal parachute troops, the Michigan national guard, and the state and city police. They were at any rate moving about.

Human limitations operate too. In a city where ordinary communications have broken down, a reporter cannot be sure of what is happening beyond the range of his eyes and ears. Things may be quiet enough where he is; but two miles away his competitors may be witnessing open warfare. Whether they are or not, someone may already have reported open warfare; and once the report has been published, no other reporter is likely to be believed by his office if he denies it. So he sets out to find it.

Yet these influences are just as well known to writing journalists. Although television journalists make their share of mistakes, both in reporting and editing the news, it would be wrong to suggest that they are any more disposed towards sensational handling of the news than anyone else. They share the standards of their peers. This does not simply mean that they have the same standards of truthfulness and public service as writing journalists: they do: many of them had their first training on newspapers. It means that they have the same view of their responsibilities as their social and educational equals in any other line of work.

A sociologist at the Center for Urban Education in New York, Herbert Gans, concluded from a series of interviews with television journalists that they were made in the image of their audience and shared its basic values. 'They do not, of course, resemble the entire audience, but its most significant segment, the young college-educated portion which is most interested in the news. . . . They are non-ideological: they lack strong political loyalties or affiliations, and choose rather to make up their minds about issues on an ad hoc basis, using the facts available to them. . . . Like the rest of the upper middle and middle class, they live in the suburbs, spend their leisure hours the same way, adopt the same fads and fashions, and read the same newspapers and mass magazines as everyone else.'

Mr Gans's findings were prepared for the Sixth World Congress of Sociology at Evian in 1966. He wrote in an American context; but his conclusions would be easy to sustain in Britain. In both countries, television news takes its special shape not from any quirk on the part of the people who put it together but from the discipline of pictures.

3 Were You There?

Because it must illustrate its reports, television has to select not merely its methods in dealing with a news event, but the event itself; and according to fairly stringent tests.

The infinite charm in television's coverage of actual happenings is that 'you are there'. When the Cardinals win the World Series or the Queen drives to open Parliament, a television set is almost as good as the best seat in the house. In fact it is almost as good as several of the best seats in the house; because you can see the expression on the pitcher's as well as the batter's face, the outside of Buckingham Palace as well as the inside of the House of Lords.

This power in television has sometimes led to the suggestion that the viewer is transported wherever important events are astir. He is not: he cannot be. He has no ticket of entry except where the event is open to cameras in conditions where they can work.

On a mechanical level television is subject to a number of technical and circumstantial hazards, notably the state of the light. More importantly, television can do very little with events of which it has no foreknowledge: although the clumsiness of its equipment diminishes every year, television can still be the slowest news-gatherer to get to work. A team of people must be assembled: power-supply, exposure, focus, sound-level must all be adjusted. Most importantly for the coverage of significant news, there are plenty of places where television cameras are not allowed in. Chief among these are the places where decisions are taken.

The mechanical problems may one day disappear. A few of them disappear each year. It is undoubtedly dispiriting, in Moscow, when the Intourist car has been located, and the gear loaded in, and the driver seized of the address, and the interview secured, and the film tin solemnly labelled 'useless if delayed' during the furious drive to Sheremetyevo airport, and the customs functionary squared, and the film bag watched into the hold of the aircraft, and the wheels seen lifting off the runway, to discover that the plane was subsequently fogbound for forty-eight hours at Helsinki. It is provoking, in New York, after film has been safely gathered in from some distant scene of conflict, and developed, and cut, and scripted, and voiced, and made ready for sending to London by transatlantic satellite, to learn that the satellite is suddenly out of use because it has been pre-empted for telephone conversations or because there has been a snow-storm at the ground station in Newfoundland. Television is increasingly proof against these accidents, but it will never be a hundred per cent proof.

The difficulty about light will have vanished when cameras can record as much as the human eye can see. Until then it will remain a nuisance. It comes up when news develops in darkness out of doors: a military manoeuvre, an accident, a demonstration. The battery-powered hand-lights which cameramen call sun-guns can illuminate a foreground; but instead of a middle distance there is blackness. The extent of the scene, the size of the crowd, is hidden. This is why there was a slightly disproportionate emphasis on fires in the television coverage of such disturbances as the one at Cleveland in July 1968. Besides being a powerful symbol of pillage and ruin, a fire is its own source of light.

The problem is seldom as intractable as it was in January 1968 when an American Air Force B-52, carrying four hydrogen bombs, crashed on the frozen sea near Thule in Greenland. The crew baled out, and all except one of them lived; but the first crew member to reach a hangar on the American air base at Thule confessed on the telephone to the Ops Room: 'We lost the bombs.' Understandably there was some anxiety to find them again. Generals and geiger-counters were flown in. A detailed search for fragments was put in hand where a long black scar on the ice seemed to show that the surface had melted and then closed over the wreck. But besides cold of more than twenty degrees below zero Fahrenheit, the enemy was darknesss. Thule is well inside the Arctic circle; and there were still three weeks of the long winter night to go before the sun would provide so much as a midday gleam of daylight.

Television reporters who went there found that they had never been so thwarted. The search itself was an astonishing sight: seven maids with seven mops mobilized for modern war – men in huge hoods made from the fur of the Canadian wolf sweeping a vast expanse of ice with instruments like vacuum cleaners. The occasion could scarcely have been more dramatic. Until it was established that all the bombs had broken apart comparatively harmlessly, the searchers were looking for four nuclear devices which had passed out of their makers' control. *Ultima Thule* might indeed become the end of the world. Even the air base was remarkable: over two thousand men gloomily defying the probabilities in stainless steel huts set on stilts, so that the snow blown off the ice cap could swirl underneath.

Yet we could take no pictures worth taking: nothing except generals' press conferences. The interest was all out of doors; and the January light never rose above the level it would only have fallen to at six o'clock in the evening in more normal latitudes. There were other, lesser problems. Camera motors jammed in the cold: such film as we shot could only be got away haphazardly, as military planes happened to be leaving for air bases in the United States. But the chief lack was light. There could have been no more effective television news blackout.

Despite the unwieldiness of its equipment and its occasional difficulties of entry, television has often been at the scene of sudden and only partly foreseeable events. In November 1963 a live camera saw Lee Harvey Oswald shot in the basement of Dallas jail. Film cameras were on the banks of Coniston Water in January 1967 when Donald Campbell's 'Bluebird' leapt out of the lake and turned over end for end. There were live cameras a few yards away in June 1968 when Robert Kennedy was shot in a Los Angeles hotel. Czech television stayed on the air in August 1968 with such pictures as it could get, and Austrian television recorded them off the air in Vienna, when Russian tanks rolled into Prague.

Yet there have been many other such events, and many momentous occasions of a less harrowing kind, where television has not been present; and here television's handicap as compared with other forms of journalism lies in the use that can be made of reconstructions after the event.

There was a television film crew within a hundred yards when Dr Martin Luther King was shot and killed in April 1968 on the open upper corridor of a Memphis motel: his visit to help in a dustmen's strike meant that the town was already in the news. Television had pictures of policemen hurrying up the stairs to the door of room 306, and of Dr King's companions in the first moments of their desolation. Radio and newspaper reporters had no advantage there. But afterwards they were able to put together increasingly detailed accounts of what had happened before they arrived: Dr King's last conversation with a musician friend about what hymn to play at that night's rally, and with his driver about whether to wear an overcoat: his murderer's surmised use of the boarding-house behind the straggling trees across the street. For television a thing only happens once. A reconstruction is no more than a series of empty places: the concrete walkway where Dr King stood, the pavement where a rifle was found.

If the problem were simply that television sometimes misses a violent death there would be no great harm done, especially since there is no evidence that television has made violence more horrifying in the process of making it more familiar. Where television's difficulty about reconstructions becomes crucial is in the reporting of occasions when decisions have been taken.

From cabinet to town council, public men dislike being watched in the process of decision. Sometimes their own cause might be hurt if the grounds for the decision became known: sometimes an opposing cause might be helped. In London there is never any formal announcement even of what was discussed at a cabinet meeting. It has to be a matter of conjecture. Senate committees in Washington may admit the press and television when they are taking soundings: never when they are taking decisions.

Journalists are not powerless in these cases. Although they do not always consult the participants as freely as they would have their public believe, they have a friend in high places. A public relations man sits in even on international discussions. The White House press man goes to cabinet meetings. The price of friendship is that he recounts the story in his own way; but the reporter can at any rate discover how long the meeting lasted and who was there.

A newspaper journalist can then present his account of the meeting in the same form as if he had been there, whatever the discrepancies in fact. Broadcast reporters have an immediate problem. If they really know what was said, why can the listener not hear it? Even more awkward, why can the viewer not see it?

The radio man falls back on the kind of story he would have written for a newspaper. The television man cannot even do that. If he simply talks to the camera, he has exhausted people's natural tolerance of that form after two hundred words. If he uses pictures of participants entering or leaving the meeting, the comings and goings of a Downing Street day, he will have enough film to say perhaps thirty words about each.

An American cabinet meeting has been televised at least once. The device was used in October 1954 to establish a fit setting for a talk to the nation on foreign affairs by John Foster Dulles, President Eisenhower's Secretary of State. It was not a complete success. Cabinet members had to ask feed questions from what appeared to be a basis of ignorance; and viewers were especially puzzled to see the President of the United States allowing himself to be lectured for nearly half an hour on what he might be presumed to know already, like some second lord in a Shakespeare history.

Genuine political activity, as distinct from amateur theatricals, is hard to televise. Television must take hold of it when it comes into the open: on journeys, at party jamborees, in certain kinds of electoral campaigning.

Journeys are very useful to television. They are international relations made visible. Television is obliged to pay attention to them. Many heads of government have discovered that it is better to travel hopefully than to stay at home. The electorate like it, to judge from the public opinion polls, because something seems to be happening. Television people like it for the same reason.

It is true that the journeys which television has most eagerly noticed as adventures in reconciliation have not often had reconciliation as their outcome; so that the notice has only increased the disappointment. The course of the Vietnam war was little changed by the Russian Prime Minister's visit to Britain in February 1967. Yet although the plan for scaling down hostilities which Mr Kosygin finally took home with him was not one he could urge with much success on Hanoi, the British government and some American officials had believed a preliminary agreement possible until opinion hardened at the White House.[1] Television could not have let the occasion go by.

The trouble with reporting contacts between nations in terms of their outward signs is that the outward signs are few and repetitive: the handshake outside the retreat where the talks are to be held, the visitor's short and guarded exposure to a curious crowd. Again and again television is driven further back yet: to the news source of last resort, the airport statement.

One of the first airport statements must have been Neville Chamberlain's at Heston airport, later Heathrow, when he got back from Munich in September 1938. 'This morning I had another talk with the German Chancellor, Herr Hitler, and here is the paper which bears his name upon it as well as mine . . .'[2] The pictures were more interesting in those days: for the newsreel cameras he stood in front of his aeroplane. Airports were too big and noisy for that by the time television was established: the talking had to be done indoors, in the airport buildings. Through these buildings in London in the sixties passed African leaders negotiating their countries' independence, and British leaders arranging armament for themselves and disarmament for other people. It was at Heathrow that the British heard their first progress reports on the attempts to penetrate the European Common Market begun in 1962 and again in 1966; and the first account of the terms proposed in December 1966 on board the cruiser *Tiger* between Ian Smith of Rhodesia and Harold Wilson. Television has reason to be grateful for the airport interview.

It is a particularly British love. Journalists in few other countries are so assiduous in questioning politicians when they are at their least clear-headed. Few airports in the world have space deliberately set aside for the purpose. If the thing is done at all it is done in the dining-room or the commandant's office. At Heathrow, in different parts of the airport, there are three specially equipped studios.

Party jamborees – conferences and conventions – are indispensable. Whatever their effect on public affairs, they are indispensable to the self-esteem and continued cheerfulness of the people who make parties work. That might not of itself be enough to keep the gatherings alive. But they are indispensable to television too. Public political speeches in the old style, directed wholly at a physically present audience, are less and less heard; but in their new form, gathered into a programme and relieved with interludes of manufactured jollity, they have become a staple of television politics.

At the beginning of this century Senator Robert LaFollette the elder would spend part of each summer travelling round his state of Wisconsin and visiting the county picnics. When the food and drink had been cleared away, and while the children played, the Senator would speak for as many as four hours. He would explain farm legislation, taxes, foreign affairs, whatever was happening in Washington; together with his own efforts to make the Republican party a Progressive rather than a Stalwart one. And if his audience heard him out, it was because they knew this would be their chief source of political information that year. However good the newspapers in rural Wisconsin at that time, not everyone would have been able to read them.

Speeches could become shorter as a politician's main channel to his electorate became the mass-circulation newspapers. He spoke to be reported. Since then the role of chief interpreter has passed successively to radio and then television. Politicians whose experience reaches back into the twenties applaud this shift to broadcasting as a bar to the newspaper monopoly which gave newspaper owners disproportionate power in the time between the beginning of general literacy and the beginning of radio. But they regret it as the end of political speech-making for its own sake. They make the point that a television audience, so far from being larger than an audience in a public place, is in a real sense much smaller: only two or three are gathered together round any one set. The speaker can look for very little communication of enthusiasm from one member of the audience to another. He will get no help from his audience either: no laughter or attentive silence to tell him that he is making his points. The first reaction he gets will be the opinion polls a month later.

The platform political speech, the address to a coughing few in an ill-lit hall, will presumably survive as long as it remains the easiest way to get into the local papers. But it is not enough for television. Television journalists realised from the outset that annual or quadrennial party gatherings at least provided a less unpromising setting.

Television coverage of the party conferences in Britain was begun by the BBC in 1955. They were joined by ITN the following year. Both sides were using film cameras. For the Labour conference at Scarborough in 1960 Granada Television, as one of the regional companies that make up the ITV network, brought in electronic cameras; though nothing was put out live. By 1962 both sides were using electronic cameras, with some live transmissions. From 1965 onward the extent of live coverage increased again.

This steady movement represented a rise in television's self-confidence and in its technical adroitness rather than in any intrinsic interest that the conferences might themselves possess. Broadcasting organisations had a variety of motives. They were covering political news in slightly more pictorial conditions than they could at other times. They were indirectly demonstrating their fitness to cover Parliament itself; and this was duly weighed when a Commons committee came to consider the question.[3] They were approaching as near as they could to the processes of political decision; and it was always possible that something genuinely worth reporting would erupt from time to time.

As laboratories for the political sociologist, the conferences have merit. There is a whole doctoral thesis in the fact that the Conservatives pray and sing a hymn: the Labour party do not pray, and their hymn – the Red Flag – is of a secular kind; while the Liberals, descended from a line of devout and vocal Nonconformists, neither pray nor sing. A good conference debate, such as the Conservatives had on Rhodesia at Brighton in October 1965, can be eloquent of a party's true nature.

On the other hand, it is difficult to maintain that the British party conferences are important in the sense that they influence subsequent events. They may be occasions to encourage the faint-hearted, or to promulgate party doctrine; yet both constitutionally and in fact they have never bound the leadership of their party. Probably the two conferences of which most public notice was taken in recent history were the Labour conference at Scarborough in 1960, when Hugh Gaitskell could not deflect his party from voting for unilateral nuclear disarmament for Britain; and the Conservative conference at Blackpool three years later, which heard Harold Macmillan's letter of imminent resignation as party leader and raised its voice in favour of Lord Hailsham instead – who at once announced that he would become Quintin Hogg again to oblige them.

Hugh Gaitskell lost no time in promising to overturn the disarmament decision, and did at the next year's conference. Lord Hailsham's candidacy had foundered on the unenthusiasm of his colleagues in cabinet even before the Blackpool conference was over.

Early in August 1968, 1333 delegates gathered at the Republican national convention in Miami Beach. More than twice that number of people went there to turn out television programmes.

In theory a convention makes a crucial choice. In fact the choice is usually made beforehand. There may be room for doubt about whether the choice will be accepted: even in 1968 the results were not utterly foregone: but on every occasion since 1956, in both parties, the candidate with the largest body of delegate support at the start of the convention has won the nomination on the first ballot.

This is not to say that conventions are not worth covering: simply that what they offer the television spectator is political emotion rather than political decision.

Even in those terms, television was unlucky at Miami Beach. On the only night that mattered there were so many honorary or diversionary candidacies that it was nearly two o'clock in the morning before Richard Nixon was finally crowned with his party's nomination. The liveliest spectacle which television could offer in normal viewing hours was mounted by a group of Hawaiians who carried placards urging other delegates to 'sing along with Senator Fong'.

Genuine emotion has flowed more freely at Democratic conventions, especially on behalf of the Kennedy family. There was powerful tension at Los Angeles in 1960 when the alphabetical roll-call of the states on the first ballot reached Wyoming before John F. Kennedy was sure of the nomination. There was an outpouring of helpless grief at Atlantic City in 1964 when Robert Kennedy was applauded for thirteen minutes before he introduced a memorial film to his brother. There was pain as well as irony at Chicago in 1968 when the memorial film to Robert Kennedy recapitulated that same scene.

Driven to cover conventions because they are available, television is lucky that they offer this much of human value. But covering conventions has very little to do with reporting politics. The decisions are not there. It is not merely that the principal decisions about who shall lead are not taken in convention cities; or if they are, they are not taken in public. There were no cameras present when Mr Nixon clinched his Southern support by assuring Senator Strom Thurmond of South Carolina that the vice-presidential choice would be inoffensive to the South. But more than that, politics is never chiefly about who leads: it is about what leaders do; and that is not decided at conventions. At Chicago the Humphrey forces had no sooner secured the Democratic convention's grudging acquiescence in President Johnson's continuance of the Vietnam war than Vice-President Humphrey himself began to indicate that he would not feel bound by the decision. It is what presidential nominees do when they become presidents that matters; and there television can seldom follow them. Television could give some account of how the Kennedy team compassed that first-ballot nomination: it could give very little account of how they compassed the withdrawal of Russian missiles from Cuba a little over two years later.

Television fastens on elections for much the same reason that it fastens on conferences and conventions – because they are there; and it has the same difficulty in distilling wisdom out of them. The decision by two successive British governments of different political persuasions, in 1962 and 1966, to try to get Britain into the Common Market was never specifically offered for argument in an election. It was potentially a decision of some significance, importing a complete change in the country's economic direction; and it was taken each time in private, in circumstances which television could neither reach nor reconstruct. Barred from witnessing decisions, television had to be content with the electoral struggles of the men who might be making them.

A body of policy is nevertheless discussed at election times; particularly, perhaps, in Britain, where party manifestoes have a longer life than American party platforms do. Television has opportunity then to document the overt topics of debate. Yet even this opportunity cannot always be taken. There is nowhere where television must be more selective than in election campaigns. It is not merely that the issues can be only allusively set out: that the advantages and disadvantages of a betterment tax on land development are not easily expounded on television. It is mainly that for a national election to be made intelligible within the compass of television it must be concentrated, epitomised. The viewer's attention must be directed to a limited number of scenes and arguments and characters – particularly characters – if he is not to lose interest in the plot altogether.

That at any rate is how British elections have so far been covered on television. It has been calculated that during the 1964 election Sir Alec Douglas-Home (as the defending Conservative Prime Minister) was quoted 70 times on television news bulletins and Reginald Maudling 26 times, with only three other Conservatives quoted as many as ten times; while Harold Wilson was quoted 83 times and George Brown 27, with only two other Labour politicians anywhere near. During the 1966 election Harold Wilson (by then Prime Minister) scored 80, George Brown 39, and James Callaghan 12 for Labour: for the Conservatives their new leader Edward Heath scored 98, Reginald Maudling 14 and Quintin Hogg 13. No one else was in double figures. Measured another way, the Wilson-

Heath argument took up more than half of all the broadcast time given to all politicians of all parties, not excluding the Liberals, the Communists and the Nationalists.[4]

The fact that this Sohrab-and-Rustum effect, this decision by single combat, had increased in the second election was especially noticeable inside television. At that time there were three television sets in the main ITN newsroom in London. One of them usually carried whatever Independent Television was offering at the time. The other two were switched on private channels to the signal from the outside broadcast units at the two main election meetings of the evening: one to Labour, the other to the Conservatives. They were raised high up on the wall, half-facing each other. People sat below them with stop-watches to select suitably fresh or matching or coherent passages. Yet that was not the quality of the raw material. The moment the two leaders appeared, usually within minutes of each other – one in Plymouth, it might be, and the other in Nottingham – they would engage in a bizarre dialogue of the deaf: apparently talking to each other, and yet not staying for an answer, not dealing with points made, not allowing for a moment that the other was a rational being. It was a strangely accurate caricature of campaign manners.

Another, lesser respect in which television is eclectic at election times is that it likes things done out of doors. A desirable element in moving pictures is movement: a crowd moves more in the open than it can on folding chairs indoors. Further, there can be no photography at all without reflected light; and natural light, being more diffused, is reflected from many more surfaces than artificial light, making more satisfyingly detailed pictures. Politicians also do more interesting things out of doors. Towards the end of the 1966 campaign Quintin Hogg, patron saint of journalists, broke a walking-stick at Turnham Green on a poster of Harold Wilson which said 'You *know* Labour government works'.

But outdoor electioneering is about the **most** wasteful of human effort that can be devised. It reaches a smaller fraction of the electorate than any other method, and in conditions less favourable to reasoned persuasion. Its chief usefulness on more than one occasion has been to find the deputy leader of a party something to do.

Television has been much better supplied with open-air campaign spectacle in America than in Britain, where (at least until 1969) election law has even forbidden hired bands. Personal contact with

a candidate is more valued in America, but constituencies at every
level have more people in them, so a simple handshake without
coherent speech is considered an acceptable gesture. Only out of
doors can hands be shaken in significant numbers. Candidates are
also more ready to fall in with the suggestions of photographers, or
even to anticipate them. During his short run as a presidential candidate in 1968 Governor George Romney took part in a game of
touch football between women undergraduates, played reveille on a
trumpet, fell out of a snowmobile and milked a cow. Television in
Britain would not collect as much outdoor political incident as that
in ten years.

There is nevertheless a kind of election in Britain which meets
some of these needs: the by-election. By-elections are in a sense television's favourite kind of election. There is often more outdoor activity than there would be in the same constituency during a general
election, simply to attract attention: by-election polls are as a rule
low, and every candidate's best hope is to get more than his ordinary
share of people to the polls. Even without these market-place and
street-corner efforts, the unity of place makes it legitimate for the
television reporter to say something of the locality and get a little
landscape into politics: the golden woods of Perthshire in the
autumn of 1963, Sir Alec Douglas-Home's new fief when he returned to the Commons as Prime Minister: the Wiltshire downs
round Devizes in the summer of 1964, where racehorse-trainers and
retired colonels held the line against revolution and first showed that
Labour's victory that autumn was not to be a romp: the grass-grown
railway-tracks of Carmarthenshire two years later, where a successful Welsh rebellion against indifference at Westminster first showed
the strength of nationalist feeling inside Britain.

Television is not alone in taking by-elections seriously. Party
leaders do it too. They have long attached to by-elections a weight
out of all proportion to the effect that the results may have on party
strengths in the Commons. When in March 1931 Stanley Baldwin
turned on Lord Beaverbrook and Lord Rothermere, whose newspapers had been calling for empire free trade, and compared them
to harlots because they wanted power without responsibility – a
defiance he could only venture on because radio had by then broken
their monopoly – his policy was considered vindicated a few days
later by Duff Cooper's by-election victory in his behalf at St

George's, Westminster. Conversely, Baldwin took the Labour capture of East Fulham from the Government at a by-election in October 1933 as a crushing vote against rearmament, and said afterwards that he could not have campaigned for it then; though Neville Chamberlain suspected that the result was simply a vote against the means test.[5]

More recent by-elections have been at least as influential. After Patrick Gordon Walker had been defeated at Smethwick in the 1964 general election, he failed to get back into the Commons at a specially contrived by-election at Leyton in January 1965, and had to resign as foreign secretary. The effect on Harold Wilson was to make him put out of his mind the March general election which he would otherwise have chosen as a means to improving his majority; and he spent the next twelve months wondering whether he had been right.

The Liberal capture of Roxburgh, Selkirk and Peebles from the Conservatives two months later was one of the chief factors in Sir Alec Douglas-Home's resignation as Conservative leader that July. A number of his followers felt that a one-time border earl ought at least to be able to hold the Borders. The votes had been declared at Jedburgh, only a few miles from the Home family acres near Coldstream.

That by-election illustrates another idiosyncrasy of by-elections which endears them to the sporting British heart: the comparatively heavy penalties exacted for failure, given the heavy attention focused on the result. As reporters waited in the gallery of the town hall where the count was held and watched the two chief candidates pacing up and down beside their rival piles of votes, it was easy to share their anxiety. This was mortal combat. Whoever lost had no visible political future. The Conservative, Robin McEwen, defending what had once been a safe Conservative seat, would incur national odium in the party if he lost it. The Liberal, David Steel, the ultimate winner, would never have a better opportunity. There were so few winnable seats for the Liberals anyway.

By-elections simplify politics: they personify and dramatise it. That is why they suit television; because television must treat politics in the same way.

4 The Interfering Eye

If television selects, it also alters. In reporting the political process it can sometimes change it.

This is received McLuhanism. 'A new form of "politics" is emerging, and in ways we haven't yet noticed. The living-room has become a voting booth. Participation via television in Freedom Marches, in war, revolution, pollution and other events is changing *everything*.'[1] In other words, television may have made political opinion-forming more sophisticated and political action less sophisticated.

The first part of this double effect, the change in the way an electorate forms its views, had been noticed less excitedly by President Kennedy while he was in the process of becoming president. Soon after his election he told a Washington reporter, Rowland Evans: 'Television gives people a chance to look at their candidate close up and close to the bone. For the first time since the Greek city-states practised their form of democracy, it brings us within reach of that ideal where every voter has a chance to measure the candidate himself.'[2]

The parallel with Greek city-states has since become a commonplace. In June 1967 the National Committee for an Effective Congress told a senate committee that 'radio and television have become the twentieth-century Athenian town square, where the public gathers, where the political contenders go to be heard, and where the citizens' decisions are formed'.[3]

Athenian voters had made things easy for themselves, all the same. The existence of a large and voteless class of women and slaves left them tolerably free to keep themselves informed. Information is the nub. Although it may seem that the holding of an instant national referendum on any topic is now only a matter of installing answer-back buttons on television sets, a modern electorate would have trouble getting the information they needed if they were to make sensible judgments on modern problems. Television could not supply all of it. Any ordinarily cautious government would refuse to supply all of it, on grounds of public safety. The usefulness of a representative assembly is not just that it is smaller than an entire electorate. In principle its members can make it their business to be better informed.

Television is doing what it can. Already it provides a great deal of raw evidence about the people in government: it has begun to provide snatches of the same service about the problems of government. A principal means to this in America, not paralleled in Britain, is the televised committee hearing.

As chairman of the Senate Foreign Relations Committee, Senator William Fulbright of Arkansas more than once deliberately used his committee as a national seminar on foreign affairs. Film and live cameras were welcomed. After Dean Rusk and George Kennan had talked to the committee about Vietnam in January and February 1966, the Senator widened the syllabus in a second set of hearings the following month. 'He brought together some of the best scholars of the nation', James Reston wrote, 'and staged the first real debate on China policy since World War II. The purpose of the hearings was not to legislate but to educate.'[4]

In February 1968 four academics took part in what the committee called an educational series on revolutions abroad; and in March Mr Rusk reappeared to spend two days repeating the arguments for the Vietnam war which he had used more than two years before.

There were hesitations in this partnership in popular instruction between television, the Senate and the administration. Not all the partners were always willing. Television gave the four academics very little exposure. Mr Rusk had dragged his feet for several months before he made his two-day reappearance; and when he did, NBC were the only network to broadcast it live.

The process also needed the co-operation of the students, the television audience. They were perhaps too well aware that television and unillustrated seminars are not wholly suited to each other. In New York a quarter of the people watching television at the time were believed to have their sets on the NBC station. It was a larger proportion than were watching any other station; but even New York is clearly a long way from Athens.

Further, not all committee chairmen are permitted to use their committee-rooms as mass classrooms. Another chairman from

Arkansas, Congressman Wilbur Mills, arbiter of the nation's taxes as chairman of the House Ways and Means Committee, might have had a large and enthusiastic extramural enrolment when he disputed the administration's reasons for wanting a surcharge on income tax. Beginning in August 1967, his committee was repeatedly visited by the top men from all the storehouses of the President's economic wisdom: the Treasury, the Federal Reserve Board, the Bureau of the Budget, the Council of Economic Advisers. The Congressman took them through the standard economic indicators, asking to be shown the signs of inflation, like a professor at a middle-western university teaching economics to a class largely made up of the football team. But viewers at large were not allowed to take the course. The House of Representatives forbids the televising of its committees.

Professor McLuhan mentioned another form of participatory democracy – the democracy of the streets: the march, the sit-in, the vigil. Television has undoubtedly had a good deal to do with the development of the form.

It cannot be maintained that there would have been no such manifestations without television. The increasing expectations of the poor in the United States, the reaction to nuclear weapons and the Vietnam war there and in Britain, demanded overt expression. At the same time, television made it seem much more pointful to bear witness in this way. If public opinion moved governments, this was the way to move public opinion: the situation complained of and the fact of the complaint were at once given wide currency.

The protest movements which became so familiar in the early sixties had their beginnings in the decade before: the boycott of the bus system in Montgomery, Alabama, in 1955 and 1956: the Easter march to the Atomic Weapons Research Establishment at Aldermaston from Trafalgar Square in London in 1958. In most ways these two enterprises were not comparable; but it so happens that they were both undertaken at a time when in each country television had reached about the same degree of development. In America in 1955 there was about one set for every six people. The same position was reached in Britain in 1958.[5] In the following nine years the proportion nearly doubled in both countries; but at one to six television was already a mass medium.

As evidence that television was a contributing cause of the original protests, this is unpersuasive. But television coverage in news bulletins undoubtedly helped the movements to grow. A way had been publicly pointed. And one of the great battlefields of the civil rights war became also a celebrated instance of the influence of television; because it published not merely the protest, but also the abuse – the cause as well as the effect.

In the autumn of 1962 Dr Martin Luther King and the Reverend Fred Shuttlesworth had decided that the Southern Christian Leadership Conference and its affiliate, the Alabama Christian Movement for Human Rights, which they led, were ready to move the following year on Birmingham. It is the largest city in Alabama: Dr King called it the largest segregated city in the United States. His aim was a measure of desegregation.

At the beginning of April 1963 successive groups of his volunteers began to sit down at lunch-counters in down-town department stores. They were arrested. Marches followed. After nine days, on Good Friday, Dr King's own arrest made the story a national one; and television crews came in to Birmingham. Birmingham Negroes had not learnt much about the doings in the town from the town's newspapers, but now they could watch them on the national news bulletins. They joined in. By the beginning of May large numbers of students were being arrested every day for protest marches. By 7 May the jails were full; but a new crowd gathered. The Birmingham police concluded that they had no recourse except to disperse it. The instruments they used, under the cold eyes of countless film cameras, were dogs and high-pressure hoses.

For advocates and opponents of Negro emancipation who saw the sight on television, it was apocalyptic. Its immediate consequences were striking enough. A truce reached in Birmingham was first wrecked by violence and counter-violence and then affirmed by the arrival of federal troops. Elsewhere in the country, from New York to Sacramento, the pattern of the Birmingham protests was re-created. Within the next ten weeks, by the reckoning of the Department of Justice in Washington, there were 758 demonstrations of various kinds across the country.[6]

Few people claimed that television was a prime cause of this first prolonged summer of unrest, except in so far as it had contributed to the realisation by the southern poor that there were other ways to live; but it was generally recognised as having been an immediate cause. The pictorial evidence had itself been an incitement. To that extent television had fathered new ways to promote change: new political methods.

It later became a common charge that television promoted disturbances where they would not otherwise have happened. In July 1967 there were four days of rioting in the suburban community of Plainfield, New Jersey. A policeman was murdered. Plainfield is just next to Newark, and the riots followed the more violent troubles there. The Mayor of Plainfield told a senate subcommittee in December 1967 that the fault was largely television's. 'The sensational coverage of the Newark riot showed persons looting stores while the police took no action to halt them. This view of looting appealed directly to the criminal and susceptible element. A mob hysteria was created which affected weak persons who would normally be law-abiding.'[7]

The Kerner Commission took a cooler view three months later. 'In some cities people who watched television reports and read newspaper accounts of riots in other cities later rioted themselves. But the causal chain weakens when we recall that in other cities, people in very much the same circumstances watched the same programmes and read the same newspaper stories but did not riot themselves.'[8]

The commission did accept the opinion that 'live television coverage via helicopter of the 1965 Watts riot had been inflammatory'. The argument would be that instant transmission makes participants more excitable and non-participants more eager to be there. As a principle it has not been proved. There were live cameras all along Main Street in Memphis in April 1968 for what was both a commemorative and an industrial demonstration the day before Dr Martin Luther King's funeral. They had no effect on the silence and order of the march.

Dr King's murder did set off disturbances in several American cities, among them Washington. Mindful of the Kerner Commission's finding that television had exaggerated the disorders of the year before, most television organisations reported them this time with such circumspection that even the police approved: in thirteen out of twenty cities surveyed by United Press International the local police department considered broadcast coverage to have been 'superior' or at least 'good'. Even in Chicago, four months later, Mr Daley did not charge television with inflaming the battles between his policemen and the forces of dissent: only with misrepresenting them by not reporting what the police had to suffer in the way of provocation – rude words, for example, such as never ordinarily fall on the ears of a Chicago policeman.

It is nevertheless clearly true that there are links between television and public disorder. Most people who take part in demonstrations of dissent are understandably aware of television. They know how widely it can publish their views. They also have some notion of what it cannot do. A few of them realise that there are one or two missiles and combat methods which television cannot show as clearly as the more obtrusive weaponry brought up by the forces of order. Many of them know that television cannot work without light.

That piece of knowledge was first turned to account in the early sixties, during France's Algerian troubles, by the Paris police; who used to go for the lights being wielded by foreign film crews and hit them out. They found it had the double effect of disarming the crew and dispersing a part of the crowd.

The point is by now widely understood. The siege of the Pentagon, the second part of the Washington demonstration in October 1967, was billed as a Saturday-to-Monday affair. The climax came just before dark on Saturday, when a few people got into the building for a few moments. After that it was over. But several people were still bivouacked on the steps of the Mall entrance and in the meadow below. The federal military police, by then in total control, made no attempt to disperse them. They put their faith in human weakness. It was a cold night, and the placards which had been the banners of the march from the Lincoln Memorial could not keep the campfires burning for long. But that by itself might not have sent the crowd away. What really sapped their spirit was that the military police passed the word among the camera teams there that if anyone put a light on, they would shoot it out; and they were believed. No one could take pictures. The watchers on the steps discovered what had happened and realised that they might just as well not be there. They could no longer make their point. By the early morning there were scarcely a hundred of them left.

Because of this interdependence, camera teams sometimes knew more about demonstrators' plans than the police did. It once fell to me to pass to the Prime Minister's senior Special Branch detective the curious message: 'They're going to stir it in the second lesson.' We were outside a Methodist church in Brighton where Harold Wilson was to read a passage from St Matthew at the start of the Labour party conference in October 1966. By then there was nothing that could be done to prevent the disturbance, which was an outburst against the British government's half-hearted support of the Vietnam war; and for all that could be heard of the second lesson, Mr Wilson might just as well have been reading from the prophet Obadiah.

The Special Branch were better prepared for a similar attempt at Scarborough the following year. A vanload of protesters were delayed before they reached the town by unexplained mechanical trouble.

If television has made a difference to elections themselves, as distinct from the less orthodox forms of democracy, it has not been in the direction of public rowdiness. Elections were rowdy already. In 1900, during the Boer War, David Lloyd George had to escape from an election meeting in Birmingham town hall disguised as a policeman.

In one simple respect broadcasting has drawn the sting from election rowdiness, and so potentially lessened it: the microphone is always with the speaker. In the October 1964 general election Sir Alec Douglas-Home, as Conservative leader and Prime Minister, spoke to over five thousand people in the Birmingham Rag Market. An unusually large part of the crowd were his opponents. He was massively shouted down. Anthony Howard and Richard West wrote in their book about that election: 'Occasionally some scraps of Home's speech floated over the din, like the sound of a single flute in a Wagner storm scene, but ninety-nine per cent was lost.'[9]

It was not lost on television. Sir Alec's great achievement – his upbringing allowed him no other course – was to keep going. The broadcasting microphones were a great deal nearer to him than they were to anybody else, and they picked up his voice without difficulty. The impression he gave on the home screen was of 'a brave man struggling in the storms of fate', and not altogether overborne by them. The hecklers were there, but so was he. There were other occasions when he was damagingly heckled; but this particular incident probably did him no harm.

Heckling is anyway very difficult for television to pick up intel-

ligibly. The hall is as a rule too large for even a directional microphone to reach the heckler's words, and too dark for a camera to
take a picture of his face. Harold Wilson, who made good use of
hecklers in that same campaign, realised that he had to repeat the
interjection before he could score off it; as when, from the floor of
Green's Playhouse in Glasgow, he was first reminded of Labour's
failed African groundnuts scheme of the late forties. 'Groundnuts?
Where have you been all this time, Rip Van Winkle?' Although
this exchange and others were sometimes repeated with the co-
operation of other audiences, it always came out on television as a
Ruth Draper performance – a duologue for one.

It may even be that for all these reasons television will in the end
do away with heckling, pointed interruptions, as a political form. It
will not be the first outward aspect of electioneering that television
has altered. Television has had an odd effect, for example, on the
details of campaign timing. It has made the end of the day the best
time to take any public step; and in the United States it has brought
the beginning of the day back into currency too. Late in 1963
Nelson Rockefeller declared his candidacy for the Republican nomination before breakfast, when there was no one else at his state
capitol in Albany except the cleaners. The gain was that he appeared
live on NBC's *Today* show.

Television has disrupted some of the oldest rituals in American
electioneering. It has become surprisingly difficult for a major candidate to meet the people: he has to reach under a camera to do it.
In October 1967, when Governor Ronald Reagan was consolidating
his claims as a possible Republican runner, he began a speaking tour
with a visit to the small town in Illinois where he had been at
college, Eureka. He was drawing strength from his roots. When he
arrived at the crossroads in front of the church which served as a
town square, the people of the town could only tell which was his
car – although it was an open one – because it was totally surrounded
by a moving mass of cameramen and sound recordists and elec-
tricians and reporters, all roped together with cables and looking like
a huge black centipede. When the Mayor climbed onto the car to
give the Governor a wooden key, the ceremony was virtually private.
The drum majorette of the school band was almost in tears: the
Governor had never even seen her.

But television has revived old rituals too. In the mid-nineteenth
century in America, particularly in the southern and western states,

two opposing candidates would often stump the country together, engaging in periodic platform debates. It saved the voters' time, and it got the candidates larger audiences than they might have attracted by themselves. In July 1858 Abraham Lincoln challenged Senator Stephen Douglas to a campaign on this pattern for the Senator's Illinois seat. Douglas agreed reluctantly: he was the better-known figure. Between August and October the two men debated in the open air in seven different towns. At Galesburg, a town of five thousand people, they drew a crowd put at twenty thousand.

As they stood, the debates would not have made acceptable television. For one thing, they were scarcely debates. One man spoke for an hour, the other for an hour and a half, and then the first man had half an hour at the end. They scarcely ever interrupted each other. The audience were quiet, too, in the early debates; though by the end the speakers were appealing for silence. The two sides were not neatly antithetic: Lincoln agreed with Douglas in opposing 'the social and political equality of the white and black races'. The result was messy: Lincoln won the popular vote, but on the indirect system then in force in Illinois Douglas held his seat.[10]

Yet the debates were widely read, and influential in Lincoln's becoming the Republican presidential candidate two years later. Television did not invent electoral debates, nor confer on them an influence that they had never had before: it re-invigorated them.

Part of television's impact on politics, therefore, has been to preserve or even revive old forms. More noticeably, though, television's reporting of political activity has itself produced new political methods: new ways, and yet not necessarily better ways, whereby citizens can study their society and seek to change it.

5 An Electronic Serjeant-at-Arms

If television has made changes in the externalities of politics, its effect also needs to be considered in the holy places, the deliberative gatherings: not just party conventions and conferences, but the United Nations, the United States Congress and the British Parliament: what it has done there, and what it might do.

It is odd that television has not made more difference than it has to the British party conferences. Because of television's interest in the occasions, three parties are presented each autumn with long stretches of broadcast time, often networked throughout the country. If programme time were for sale in Britain the cost would run into millions. Yet the parties, with commendable scruple, make almost no attempt to regulate what goes on the air in their name. Their least creditable figures parade freely. The first British party which determinedly controlled its party conference product on television would reap enormous benefit. The benefit would not last: the other parties and the television organisations would catch up; but there would at least be a gain in the sophistication of political propaganda.

In June 1965 Timothy Beaumont, later Lord Beaumont, said as head of the Liberal party organisation in a letter to a Commons committee: 'We have found that the presence of cameras in the conference hall has made no difference to the running of the conference, except in the one or two cases when the managers of the conference, knowing that a particular debate was being televised, have chosen which delegates should speak.'[1] No one would have known that there was even this degree of manipulation. Many Liberals still remember an unhappy afternoon at Brighton in September 1963, when live television time during the big debate of the assembly was successively occupied by some of the party's least persuasive candidates for Parliament. Yet there was indignation in the party when

Jo Grimond suggested at the private business session of the assembly three years later, his last as party leader, that it might be useful to stage-manage things a little better.

The recorded view of the other two parties is that television has made little impact.[2] Dark glasses on the platform, perhaps, because of the lights – and even there the Conservatives have been stoically resistant: nothing much else.

Some individual politicians have disagreed. During the Commons debate in November 1966 when the idea of a television experiment was defeated by a single vote, Quintin Hogg said: 'The standing ovation is a post-television institution in both party conferences.... I must say that I detest the standing ovation even when I receive it. It is a lamentably undemocratic and sycophantic thing.'[3] This surprised those Conservative members who had seen him at Blackpool in 1963, since if conference applause could have made a prime minister he would have become one then.

Another speaker in the same debate who deplored these ovations thought they arose from the need to show the viewers a united party. But the semblance of unity is all that party conferences have ever aimed at. There would have been more ground for complaint if the atmosphere thus broken into had been one of earnest and informed striving after the best policy for the party. No one claimed that it had been.

It would be difficult to show that American party conventions have become more demonstrative since television moved in on them. The frenzy on Wendell Willkie's behalf in 1940 was by all accounts at least as noisy as the nostalgic outburst for Adlai Stevenson in 1960.

The remarkable thing about the conventions is how little they too have been affected by television. The hall is a little more cluttered, and the lights are a little brighter. The Democrats banned snake-dancing in the aisles at Chicago in 1968 because the amount of it televised from Miami Beach had made the Republicans look a little foolish. But conventions are no more open than they were before television to the kind of instant popular pressure that television might be expected to generate.

Imperfect though it is, the American method of choosing party leaders is at least as responsive to the general will as the British method, where the choice rests entirely with members of Parliament

elected for quite other purposes and chiefly conscious of the needs of
the central government. A system of state delegations takes some
account of local anxieties. Politicians left at home are mainly anxious
that their state delegation should be on the side of the man who wins
the nomination, in order that the state should stand a chance of
subsequent presidential favours. Television purports to give an
instant account of movements of opinion at the convention. On this
information the watchers by the hearth can pester their representatives to fall in behind whoever appears to be in the lead. A bandwagon can start to move.

Both at Miami Beach and Chicago television had a ready-made
opportunity to create this kind of effect and did not altogether reject
it: yet nothing happened. In both parties the choice of the party
hierarchy was a figure who commanded only reluctant and unenthusiastic loyalty from most of the rank and file. In both parties
there were more presentable contenders with a better chance of
beguiling the electorate at large. At both conventions the American
networks busily reported the claims made and the activity undertaken on behalf of these men: notably on behalf of Senator Edward
Kennedy at Chicago. The delegates could see what was being said
on television: many of them were watching portable television sets
where they sat, and some had little other source of information. The
people whom they represented were watching television too. Delegates could be reached by telephone even in their seats. Yet when
the dust had settled and the votes had been counted, nothing had
changed. Mr Nixon and Mr Humphrey had almost exactly the
same number of delegate votes as their managers had claimed for
them.

Even in detail the American television networks are innocent of
the influence over convention arrangements that they are sometimes
credited with. In 1967 they waged a long campaign to persuade the
two major parties to hold their 1968 conventions in the same city,
in order to save the cost of moving the television equipment from
one place to another – which for one network had been over a million dollars in 1964. When the Republicans settled on Miami Beach
for 1968, the networks let it be understood that they would not be
able to cover the Democratic convention in colour unless the Democrats too went to Miami Beach. President Johnson called their
bluff. He took the view that the state of Illinois was more important
to his party than the state of Florida, and he chose Chicago. The

next day the networks discovered that they would after all be able to cover the Democratic convention in colour.

The United Nations cannot be said to have been altered by television, since the organisation grew up with it. Emplacements for film and television cameras were built high into the walls of the three council chambers as well as of the general assembly hall itself. The UN television unit takes its own pictures even when nobody else does.

Partly because the cameras are hidden, and partly out of the pervasive anxiety to take the thing seriously and make it work, UN television coverage is very discreet. There is no dalliance with detail. You would never discover by watching television, for example, how many good-looking women move softly about its carpeted spaces. But in any case the UN is the kind of institution that has nothing to fear from television. Its public purpose is declamatory rather than deliberative. Any real negotiating is done out of the camera's range.

The number of legislatures televised is still small. In continental Europe, French experience was briefly added to Dutch, Scandinavian, Italian and West German while the Office de Radiodiffusion Télévision Française was free of government control during the turmoil of May 1968. In the United States the practice has never spread beyond a handful of state legislatures, and even there restrictedly: Oklahoma, Missouri, New York, New Mexico. The United States Senate, which likes to be known as the greatest deliberative assembly in the world, has never been televised. Sternly edited, it might produce very good television, with its rules which allow members to talk directly to each other and in effect to discuss what they like. There would be technical problems: members wander about and often talk very quietly, in the confidence that the shorthand writer is following them.

The House of Representatives is never televised as such either. But the two Houses of Congress sometimes assemble together to hear eminent men, and they use the House chamber, as being the larger of the two. These occasions are open to television. They have commonly been reserved for presidents reading their state-of-the-union message, or for generals home from the front. It was at such a televised joint session in April 1951 that General Douglas MacArthur, dismissed by President Truman from his American and UN commands in Korea, reminded the nation that old soldiers never died. His own resulting moment in the sun lasted about six weeks.

The chairman of a senate committee may decide to admit either no outsiders at all; or newspapermen only, with the lay public; or the full array of public and press and radio and television. If television is excluded, the cameras are often set up in the corridor outside, and witnesses are taken through their testimony again when they emerge; but even that the chairman may discountenance. If television is allowed in, a witness may get immunity from it, if he makes a case; but the chairman must first have decided to observe some such rule as is used by the Senate's Permanent Subcommittee on Investigations: 'A witness may request, on grounds of distraction, harassment, or physical discomfort, that during his testimony, television, motion picture and other cameras and lights shall not be directed at him, such request to be ruled on by committee members present and voting at the hearing.'[4]

The great difference between a committee of either House of Congress and a committee of the House of Commons is that a congressional committee can originate legislation as well as pass upon it; and to help it do this, it can call people of experience in the given field to offer evidence. A committee chairman may therefore have one of a number of purposes in mind when he holds hearings: he may simply want a problem ventilated, he may be wondering about bringing in legislation, or he may firmly intend to produce a bill out of one or more proposals in front of him. The practice has been that he excludes television the moment the time comes for the members of the committee to stop listening and start talking themselves.

In Britain and America, this is still the crucial divide. Political assemblies are televised only as far as they are not deliberative. When they have an issue of substance to decide, the bar comes down. Television is held inimical to decision.

This is the pith of the argument against televising the House of Commons. When the Commons television experiment was debated and narrowly defeated in November 1966, a number of insubstantial arguments were advanced against the idea: as that the technicians would take over, or that the place would become a performing-flea circus.[5] The substantial arguments were not heard in that debate; but they had been heard in an earlier debate in May 1965. Aidan Crawley, then a Conservative backbencher, maintained that Commons debates were 'neither entertainment nor instruction. . . .

Our debates are not geared to television.'⁶ J. J. Mendelson, following him from the other side of the House, developed the point: 'Parliament always has been and always will be a parliamentary workshop. It is the passing of new legislation and the imposition of new taxes and the appropriation of expenditure which are the heart of parliamentary work. These matters are, in the nature of the case, very often the subject of quiet, long-winded discussion.'⁷

Mr Mendelson was afraid that this workshop function would be obscured by the way television editors chose their material. But he also identified the other danger, which is that members themselves 'would more and more become concerned about what the cameras were recording'; and this might make them more concerned about the effect they were having on the viewer than on the matter in hand. There is a third possibility: that the workshop function would simply be pushed back into some untelevised stage of Commons proceedings. This happened to local councils in Britain once they were obliged by law to let the press in: solid deliberation was moved out into committees and party caucuses, and the full council merely ratified the result. There is still solid deliberation in the Commons, particularly in the kind of empty house in which Mr Crawley and Mr Mendelson spoke. It is possible that the cameras would drive it upstairs into the committee rooms, never to return.

But this did not seem to be the reason why 131 members voted against even the idea of an experiment and about another 370 did not vote at all, effectively ruling it out for the life of that parliament. What troubled many MPs was the fear that the uninstructed viewer might not like what he saw.

Every parliamentary reporter remembers the astonishment of his first visits to the press gallery. It will not have been empty benches that surprised him, though members sometimes affect to believe that outsiders are puzzled by all that untenanted green leather. No voter who thought about it for a moment would expect his representatives to sit and listen to each other all day. The reporter's main impression is more likely to have been formed when the House was fairly full: in the early afternoon, for question-time and ministers' statements.

What strikes the fresh witness then is the close parallel with the atmosphere of a boys' boarding-school; and not a very good boarding-school at that. The parallel is not new: it was elaborated in a *roman-à-clef* published under a pseudonym by Dr Donald Johnson while he was still Conservative member for Carlisle.[8] But it hits off an atmosphere into which even Labour members not born to those disadvantages, even women members, seem cheerfully to fit. There is the noise, for one thing. No mob of well-born urchins waiting for the lunch bell or jumping up and down on a touch-line could produce more. Linked to this is the factitious animosity between the two sides. Members of the opposing parties, like the inmates of School House and Inkerman House, or even boarders and day bugs, have many more common than conflicting interests, if they could read them right; but to keep up their spirits in an uncertain world they need to claim that inherent superiority can proceed from accidental classifications.

There are the jokes which convulse an entire chamber and leave the public gallery, the Speech Day visitors, stony-faced. There are the taboos: step across a line in the carpet or mention the House of Lords and you are shouted at as if you had worn your boater in the tuck shop. Only frontbenchers may read their speeches: only monitors may leave undone the bottom button of their waistcoats. The captain of the cricket team must never be referred to as such, but as the keeper of the bats: Enoch Powell must never be referred to as Enoch Powell, but as the right honourable gentleman the member for Wolverhampton South-West; and for those members who cannot remember the South-West, which is a good many, the lapse will be filled by *Hansard* in the morning.

It might be thought the influence of architecture. The mid-nineteenth century, when the Houses of Parliament were rebuilt, was the great growth period for British boarding-schools: many of them share its oppressive style. New members have a half-forgotten pattern of behaviour at once suggested to them. But these patterns are older than the nineteenth century. Members have been conducting themselves like this since the Restoration. On one occasion in the middle of the eighteenth century a member was demanding of another where the evidence for a certain claim was to be found. He more than once used the phrase 'Let him tell me where'. Two members near him at once began to sing a song then in favour in London which used those last three words as a refrain: William Boyce's 'Tell me, lovely shepherd, where'. The merriment was colossal.

Granted that these modes are not new, it might conceivably be useful to show them to a wider audience than the few thousand people who now pass through the Commons public gallery each year. Television might inhibit this side of Commons life at least as surely as its quiet workshop side.

The Lords experiment of February 1968 could not provide evidence on this. Peers have long been immensely polite to each other. They can afford to be: not much power is at issue. In the three days of the test they showed their capacity for knowledgeable and unembarrassed discussion of practically anything: savings banks on the first day, sport on the second, 'street offences' by predatory males on the third. The outcome was shown on closed circuit inside the Palace of Westminster, first live and then edited. Some five months later a House of Lords committee recommended that Lords proceedings should be available for radio and television whenever the broadcasting authorities were interested. A number of other decisions were still needed before the recommendation could be ratified. But its unassertive terms showed that their lordships recognised the real obstacle: the men in charge of news broadcasting had to put their limited money where the news was, and that was not the House of Lords.[9]

Television's parliamentary opportunities are better than they were. At least the fourteen-day rule is dead – though that was a restriction which operated outside the Palace of Westminster rather than inside it. The rule forbad broadcast discussion of any topic that was to be debated in either house within a fortnight. The BBC were held to it for many years by an agreement with the political parties, and it was made a formal government instruction in 1955 when ITV began. It was dropped in December 1956, nearly six years after the Beveridge Committee report on broadcasting had recommended that it should be.[10]

It was one absurdity removed. Several remained. For one thing, there was nowhere for television people to work. In Washington a television reporter can come straight out of the House or Senate gallery and talk to an electronic camera about what he has seen and heard. It may not be television, but it is reporting. At Westminster this can be done for radio: the BBC have a gothic telephone-box got up as a one-man studio in their office behind the Commons press gallery: but not for television. They have a small single-camera studio across the road, under the walls of the Abbey: it is believed to have been the Dean's air-raid shelter. ITV, late in 1968, still had no permanent installations nearer than their studios in Kingsway, over a mile down the river.

For the early evening news programme at five minutes to six, when traffic was heavy, the quickest way to cover the distance was by underground. At Westminster it was easy to reach the tube from New Palace Yard; but from Temple Station at the other end there was still about a third of a mile to be covered, mostly uphill. It often happened that the principal opposition speaker in a major debate had not even made his main point by half past five.

When either television news organisation wanted more space or readier contact with parliamentarians, they had to improvise a studio in the Westminster neighbourhood. On one cold night the BBC grouped a collection of MPs round a brazier in Parliament Square. On Budget Days ITV regularly hired the second floor of the St Stephen's Tavern, a public house in Westminster Bridge Road. During the Chancellor's speech, breathless reporters would arrive from the press gallery with late word – very late word – of how the House was taking it: news of the actual budget changes had already been relayed from telephones behind the press gallery to the main Kingsway studio. After the speech, MPs would climb the tavern steps to offer judgments.

More time to report did not necessarily bring greater ease. For five years ITN had a weekly programme on Parliament called *Dateline Westminster*. Its raw material was simply speeches that had been made in both Houses during that week. The problem was how to render them. For a while quotations from speeches were read by radio actors behind still pictures of the speakers; but later the suspicion grew that the actors were imitating the politicians instead of just quoting them, and the reporters who delivered the linking passages took over the speeches too. Even the illusion of a reconstruction had proved difficult to sustain.

An earlier programme, *Questions in the House*, put out by Associated-Rediffusion from 1960 to 1962, had found it necessary to cut the knot by reporting on Parliament in terms of issues that could be covered away from Parliament altogether: the meadow road in Oxford, the independence of Rutland.

All these obstacles to efficient parliamentary reporting for television are not in themselves arguments for trundling the cameras in. Many of the difficulties could be put right more easily than that. But they would be much lessened if some limited coverage were allowed. And this could be done without interfering with the workshop function. Formalised occasions like Budget Day could be televised with no more interruption of the routine than has been occasioned by televising the state opening of Parliament, or the state-of-the-union message in Congress. The coverage could perhaps be extended to those general debates where legislation is not in question, on foreign affairs or defence. It might even be stretched to take in parts of question-time.

Question-time is what television journalists would most like to get at. It has a large cast, frequent changes of pace and mood, and a livelier script than most other parts of the parliamentary day. But within the House there has for some years been concern about question-time. Many members believe that their rigid ration of one substantive and one supplementary question on any topic makes ministerial evasion too easy. Some MPs would feel that the public witness of television would strengthen the backbencher's hand here. Others would take the view that television has already borrowed too much of the private member's power to question the minister, and ought not to encroach further.

In February 1964, with a general election certain for that year and expected in the spring or early summer, there was some disquiet among Labour opposition leaders at the idea that they were getting less opportunity to question the Prime Minister than television journalists were.[11] But as Ronald Butt has pointed out in his book *The Power of Parliament*, television interviewers ask a different kind of question, and from a different level. They are trying to elicit fact, not to promote opinion. They cannot be as denunciatory as parliamentary questioners. Question-time and political interview programmes are not in competition.[12]

Further, question-time is more precious to opposition than to government backbenchers; and it is a matter of observation that an opposition benefits more from television coverage of its clashes with authority than a government does, because television will give an opposition proportionately more space than newspapers do.[13] A newspaper is principally interested in the fact of the government's action. A television account of the exchange would be interested in that too, but it would give almost equal prominence to the fact of the opposition's disagreement. For this reason, television coverage of question-time would probably stiffen the arm of the people who use it most, the opposition.

There is always a tendency for an opposition, feeling itself oppressed or unfairly overborne, to look on television as its due recourse. Both in Britain and America this has made the chief opposition party very assertive of its rights in the period before any election that looks like being closely fought. In January 1968 the Republicans demanded an equal allowance of time to reply to President Johnson's state-of-the-union message, and got it. But even in a country where political time can be freely bought, no sustained attempt to keep an opposition going on television has so far worked. The 'Ev and Charlie Show', which began in March 1961 – Senator Everett Dirksen and Congressman Charles Halleck presenting the Republican view as minority leaders in the two Houses of Congress – was never more than a weekly press conference excerpted by the television news shows, and it probably won more ridicule than votes. After Congressman Gerald Ford had replaced Mr Halleck in January 1965, the 'Ev and Gerry Show' as even more episodic in its appearances.

Winston Churchill more than once advocated introducing into Britain the American system whereby politicians could buy broadcast time. He first broached the idea in December 1929, only seven years after the beginning of sound broadcasting in Britain. Sir John Reith, the BBC's Director-General, replied that – aside from the fact that the Corporation's licence forbad it – such a system operated 'irrespective of any consideration of content or balance'. Churchill retorted that he preferred it to 'the present British methods of debarring public men from access to a public who wish to hear'. He was in opposition at the time: but he was chiefly anxious to advertise his general policy differences with his own party leader, Stanley Baldwin.[14]

Perhaps that is the parliamentary role that broadcasting can most readily serve in: as a vehicle for internal opposition within a party. Resigning ministers have often used it as such. When Ray Gunter in July 1968 gave up his post as Minister of Power in the second Wilson government, he made no Commons resignation speech at all. He appeared on a succession of radio and television news programmes instead.

Television has not so far progressed beyond these peripheral ministrations to deliberative bodies. The cameras are only allowed inside when they offer useful advertisement without the threat of change. They are excluded from almost every assembly where decisions importing action are likely to be taken. These are not the conditions for the comprehensive gathering of news.

PART III

Television and Leaders

6 Say a Few Words

Television has to take what it can get. It prefers pictures, but not all the situations it must report are cast in a pictorial mould. In the coverage of politics it must often be content with politicians talking. But it cannot as a rule get to them when they are talking for their primary purpose, which is to reach agreement on national or international action. It must accept peripheral talking. Much of this peripheral talk is specially arranged by television for itself; in the form of that indispensable of broadcasting, the interview.

This is another kind of television coverage which may alter what happens simply by setting out to report it. Since the birth of speech by interview is induced rather than natural, public men sometimes say more to a questioner than is wise or intended; and this can at least speed the course of events.

For reasons which are mostly to do with the organisation of television, this pressure can be heavier in Britain than in America.

Most politicians depend ultimately on the favour of an electorate. Television seldom needs to pay politicians for appearing: the only honorarium it need offer them is exposure to their own voters. It is an article of faith with all politicians, and one incapable of disproof, that to appear on television is to win votes; and conversely, that if there is no opportunity to win votes it is almost pointless to appear on television. A senator's assistant once said to me, kindly but firmly, to explain the unlikeliness of his master's giving me an interview: 'How many of your viewers have votes in Idaho?'

When a British politician goes on television, he has much more certainty than an American politician has of being seen by his own voters. This makes him in general more disposed to yield to television reporters who want to ask him questions.

In Britain his basic political security, his constituency, is not a large area: perhaps only a few square miles, never more than three small counties and depopulated at that: a unit in principle of about sixty thousand people. The signal must reach that area, and it must do it either from a local or a national source.

If he is appearing on the local television service which commands his constituency, he has no problems. The regions into which the BBC and the Independent Television Authority divide their empires are extensive, and there are very few constituencies which do not fall wholly within one or another. But in the United States there are ten states, counting Alaska, which each have a larger surface area than the whole of the United Kingdom. Taken together with the fact that American local television stations have a shorter range than British, this means that there are at least twenty senators who cannot hope to reach even a significant proportion of their voters in a single local appearance. They have that much less eagerness to appear.

This applies at lower levels than senator. The state of Wyoming is just larger than the United Kingdom. But congressmen, unlike senators, are apportioned roughly on a population basis; and Wyoming only rates one congressman. Great numbers of congressional districts spread beyond the reach of a single television station.

So for many American politicians the only way to be seen on a news programme by a useful proportion of the audience that matters to them is to be seen on nationally networked television. To get attention locally they have to deserve it nationally. They know that this may not happen to them often.

Politicians spend most of their time in the capital. A British politician accosted by a television crew in London tends to take it for granted that the result will be networked. Not much television news is put out from London for purely local consumption: the parochialism of the capital leads journalists working in London to suppose that what interests them will interest the country. A British cabinet minister once gave a live television interview in London on ITV and then rang his wife, knowing she watched nothing else, to ask her how he had done. 'But you weren't on, dear,' she said. It turned out that the interview had only gone to the North-East. His constituency was in the Midlands. There was a painful scene.

In Washington no American politician could have been so sure in the first place. There is a great deal of local television activity, and very little assurance of national distribution. The congressman from Wyoming waylaid in Washington may suspect that none of the microphones in front of him are from the networks, and may be certain that none are from KFBC-TV, Cheyenne. Which may be enough to strengthen him to say 'No comment'.

This extra influence for British television springs from its geographical advantages. A more powerful influence comes from its organisational advantages. Because there are basically only two television bodies in Britain, there are many more occasions than in America when a politician is interviewed by a single questioner.

On most news occasions in Britain there are only two cameras or sets of cameras there: one each from some branch of the BBC and of ITV. With only two crews engaged, it is usually possible to persuade the object of interest to be questioned twice, separately and successively. Established by ITN when commercial television began in Britain in September 1955, the pattern survived. Most people accepted it because they had no other experience to judge it by. This was how television behaved. Politicians accepted it because they needed the goodwill of television people: they swallowed the technical argument that an interview would be untidy if the speaker kept turning his head between two questioners, and disquieting if he looked at neither of them; and they liked the idea that if they made a mess of the first bite at the cherry they could have another one, so that at least half the nation should judge them rightly.

For broadcasting journalists it introduced a new and irrelevant skill into the business of interviewing: the decision whether to go first or second. It was often settled with a coin, but it could be manipulated. There were some public figures, like Field-Marshal Lord Montgomery, whose first, fine, careless response was the only one worth having. Similarly there were times when men could not convincingly reproduce their first flash of indignation at some charge which the reporter had to level. On the other hand there were figures – one or two princes of the church come to mind – who were pithier the second time round; and it was sometimes useful to see what a man had to say before deciding what to ask him.

This double-interview procedure was not invariable. There might be more. There might be an extra one for BBC radio, if the BBC's television reporter had not held a microphone for radio as well; or if the client was a cabinet minister there might be a deferential one for the Central Office of Information. For many years the COI used a microphone concealed in an ornate gilt inkstand, like a Moscow listening device. Other BBC and ITV programmes besides the news might also be engaged. At the end of the Commonwealth Prime Ministers' Conference in London in September 1966 Harold Wilson gave eleven successive broadcast interviews of various kinds: five for overseas networks, three for the BBC, two for ITV and one for the COI. More ordinarily, though, if the number of applicants rose above two or three there would be one general interview, like a small press conference; and the same thing happened if the conditions were hurried in some way.

The normal pattern remained successive duologues. Now a duologue has two sides, whatever the differences in standing. It is begun and continued by agreement. When a politician and a television reporter sit down together, each is doing something special for the other. The politician is giving of his time and thought. The reporter, as his employers' representative, is making available considerable technical resources for the translation of that thought into widespread political information. It is a semi-contractual relationship.

If the contract were written out, it would say that each party agreed as far as he could to make the other's expenditure of effort worthwhile. The reporter's side of the bargain is very simple: he will try to see that the material gets on the air. He cannot promise this, because there are too many variables; but he knows that his employers are disposed to use the interview, he will try to ask the questions in such a way as to sustain their interest, and he will do what he can to get the material favourably looked at by the editors of the day.

The politician's unspoken undertaking is more delicate. It is to say something usable. He need not sparkle; but he must say something just fresh enough to carry the story a little further. If he returns from negotiating with an African government, sits down in front of the camera at the airport, waits until the cameraman has said 'running' and the reporter has put a question, and then announces that he can say nothing about his journey until he has reported to Parliament, there will not be a crew to meet him next time. It is an irreproachable answer; but he ought not to be in the chair at all. He has entered into an agreement and broken it at once.

Most British politicians may not have formulated this rule of procedure, but they observe it. The danger for politicians is that they will observe the rule too well. In their anxiety to say something that will be broadcast, even if they do not see it as the fulfilment of a contract or an insurance against ill-will, they may say something that will return to plague them.

In July 1966 Mr Wilson was off for a weekend in Moscow. Part of the point of the trip was to show his tirelessness in peace-making: the visit had been planned at the time of a crisis on the Labour backbenches over British support for America in Vietnam. But in the interval that crisis had been replaced by a graver one about sterling and Britain's balance of payments. The government were to announce measures to meet it as soon as the Prime Minister got back. Slightly to the surprise of his staff, he agreed to give me a television interview at the airport as he left. It was unavoidable that he should be asked whether there would be time to do a sensible job on the impending cuts with the head of the government out of the country. He said there would; that unlike Conservative moves in the past, this would not be a hurried scraping-together of panic measures; and that it would work. The claim might have been justified historically, but it was not justified by events, and it was much used against him.

This particular peril, arising at least partly from a habit of single interviews, is much less present in the United States. In June 1967 there were 970 television stations on the air across the country. They were supplied with material by three major networks and a number of subsidiary sources, as well as by their own staffs. This made it unlikely that at any foreseeable happening of current interest there would be as few as two cameras engaged. Half a dozen was a much more probable number. There would also be at least as many radio stations represented from among the 6519 then in being.[1]

In face of a dozen microphones, the only practicable method was the general statement. It might be touched off by a question, and it might be followed by more; but it would need to answer no more than the highest common factor of journalistic curiosity, and no one would feel that there was any necessity 'either to tell or to hear some new thing'.

There are, of course, encounters *à deux* on American television; and it was during one of them that there occurred the classic instance in recent American politics of a self-inflicted injury during a television interview. Governor George Romney, explaining on a suburban Detroit station in September 1967 why he had once approved the Vietnam war, said of his visit to South Vietnam nearly two years before: 'I just had the greatest brainwashing that anybody can get when you go over to Vietnam: not only by the generals, but also by the diplomatic corps over there – and they do a very thorough job.'

Although, in deference to the local fame of the interviewer, the programme was called *Lou Gordon/Hotseat*, Mr Gordon said nothing either to provoke the term 'brainwashing' or to explore it. Even the public relations man who came with the Governor to the recording saw nothing that needed modification. He found out from the newspapers after the interview had been transmitted three days later.

The effect of the phrase Governor Romney had used was to epitomise his intellectual weaknesses cruelly. A man who could be brainwashed by American military men, and confess it, was convicted of a double simplicity of mind. The Governor could not anyway have long remained the leading contender for the Republican presidential nomination, as he then was: his propensity for verbal clumsiness rapidly became too marked: yet that moment under the studio lights of WKBD-TV at Southfield, Michigan, did more than anything else to hasten his decline.

Lou Gordon was unusual in being alone with his victim. The panel formula is much more regularly used in American studios: one man to answer the questions, three or four to ask them.

This arrangement has again and again saved public men. It should be held axiomatic that television questioning is effective in inverse proportion to the number of questioners. The more voices, the fewer answers. Yet television producers delight in the formula. The impression they believe it gives is of no effort being spared to get at the truth. The more eminent, the more numerous the inquisitors the better. When one of them flags, another leaps over his exhausted body to continue the fearless probing.

It seldom happens. NBC reduced the formula to absurdity when they arranged special editions of *Meet the Press* in August 1968 in which six newspaper owners or editors confronted Governor Rockefeller before the Republican convention and Vice President Humphrey before the Democratic. Neither politician ever had an easier ride. Newspaper moguls are more in the habit of answering questions than asking them. The technique works scarcely better in the form used in Britain, where a questioner need not wait for the chairman's nod. In January 1967 the editors of two daily and two weekly newspapers, with an equally eminent moderator, were flown from London to Washington to question Dean Rusk for Indepen-

dent Television about the continued justification for the Vietnam
war. It was to be a showdown: tough, final. During the hour that
they talked to him, the Secretary of State never had to do more than
placidly rehearse known American positions.

The formula comes to grief on scruples and rivalries. The well-
mannered members of a group are unwilling to hog the questioning,
and the ill-mannered ones interrupt other questioners anyway.
They are interrupted in turn by the chairman. In any event no line
of questioning can be pursued. The great man only needs one fallback position on each difficult issue. He will not be asked to defend
it. Nothing much can be concerted in advance, because if the questions are to tread on any new ground at all then there can be no
certainty what the answers will be. Every member of the group is
very conscious of the clock. An hour, perhaps even half an hour:
take out time for the advertisements: allow perhaps four-fifths of
what is left for the answers; and even the residue, the time for questions, has to be divided by five. Out of half an hour it leaves a ration
of a minute a head. Since this is clearly absurd, questioners are
tempted to increase their share by asking very long questions. Long
questions evoke long answers: no remedy there. The situation is
made worse because in any group there will be one or two questioners who are less practised than the rest. They may well be the
best-informed people there, but they will make mistakes. They will
become bogged in specialist points: they will ask questions which
invite mere assent and so allow an extended answer on something
else: they will not be ready with the obvious objections; and so on.
The formula is very hard to use effectively.

A more real scourge of statesmen in Britain is the surprise interview: sometimes called a doorstep, or even a jump. This too is much
less common in the United States; again, as a consequence of the
plethora of cameras. If the story is so interesting that a figure at the
centre of it is worth lying in wait for, other people will have thought
of it too. The street will be full of cameras. Surprise is already out
of the question; and if anyone is to get anything, there must be joint
organisation. The end result is a 'stake-out': a collection of meek
and stationary microphones which can easily be snubbed.

Not so easily in Britain, because there are only two of them at
most, and in the hands of agile and persistent reporters. If the great
man only has to cross a pavement from a doorway to his car, the

chase is too short to put him in much danger; but if the terrain is more open there may be more incident. The high summer of this technique was during the Profumo troubles in 1963, when the Macmillan government was embarrassed by a war minister who seemed to have shared a mistress with a Russian naval attaché and who misled the Commons about it. Because Downing Street was being refurbished, the cabinet met at Admiralty House, which has a wide, enclosed courtyard giving on Whitehall. There were mornings when it looked like a bear-pit. In the end the cameras were asked to stay away.

If there was any skill in this kind of interviewing, it lay in starting with a question which was easy to answer and difficult not to answer. If the subject broke step to reply, a dialogue had begun. My own classic of fatuity in this genre was 'Glad to be back in London, Mrs Kennedy?' delivered under a policeman's arm when the President's wife was on a visit in March 1962. It gave good results.

It was a little while before public figures discovered that there was absolutely no contract implicit in this kind of encounter. They were not obliged to say a thing. Yet they continued to drop unconsidered trifles in doorways and have trouble with them afterwards. The doorway of Ten Downing Street was a favoured place. When the Labour government was being put together after the 1964 election, Charles Pannell hesitantly revealed beside the railings that he had got the job he wanted, the ministry of public buildings and works. He was not the only minister to disclose his new job, but he never recovered from an impression of gaucherie created at just the time when Labour were anxious to demonstrate that they knew the score as well as anybody else. He did not survive into the second Wilson government.

As a final point, it does seem to be broadly true that television interviewers in Britain are prepared to be tougher and more hostile than they are in America. This is at any rate the common finding of American correspondents in London.[2] There are plenty of exceptions here, and no possibilities of proof; but it is in general another respect in which television leans on public men in Britain a little more heavily than in America.

An American newspaper reporter is trained in the journalism of fact. He presents his readers with the raw material for a judgment; not with the judgment itself. That is for columnists, a separate branch of the profession. Newspaper reporters in Britain and most other European countries are more interested in the journalism of opinion. They are anxious not merely that you should know what happened but that you should know what to think about it.

These long-standing traditions in its parent profession have spilled over into television journalism. When American television reporters interview a politician, they want their viewers to know what he thinks. British television reporters want it known what they think as well.

This is the main reason why television journalists in Britain are so chary of allowing a politician his say without objection or intervention. They are not so much concerned with fairness to his opponents as with fairness to themselves. They dislike having it thought that they are ignorant of the arguments on the other side.

American television men are less sensitive on this point. Many American provincial television stations cannot afford to be sensitive on it. If a politician fills a hole for nothing, they will put him on, due counter-arguments or not.

There are two basement studios under the Capitol in Washington where members of Congress make videotaped reports to their electors. If they use an interlocutor at all, he may well be on the member's staff. One senator used to pay journalists $50 to ask the questions; but it was understood that they would not be asked to ask them again if their attitude was in any way evaluative. The stations to which the videotapes are sent screen them gratefully in the dead hours of Sunday afternoon, and claim credit for public spirit into the bargain.

Interviews with politicians can of course be emollient in Britain and abrasive in the United States, but not as a rule. When interviewers on American television are tough, it is sometimes with the active complicity of the man they are interviewing. Before his 1968 campaign Richard Nixon constantly acted on the belief that he would become an object of sympathy if he were interviewed by 'the toughest reporters in town'.

In Britain the custom has been commoner and more spontaneous. George Brown was charged on television in August 1966 with having appropriated the foreign secretaryship as his price for not resigning from the government altogether at a damaging moment for the economy: in October 1967, a few months before he did resign, he was asked about how much he drank. This does not arise out of any claim about equality between politicians and journalists in Britain. American reporters may well have an easier relationship with politicians, and American columnists more influence on them. It arises from an anxiety that the due objections should be put.

The practice can spring from other causes as well: from a wish to make a reputation, or from the needs of entertainment. There are politicians who coruscate if they can be made to lose their temper. It probably does little harm. For every difficult encounter a politician will have several easy ones; and even the difficult one may win him sympathy, on the old Nixon plan. Tough television interviews, like television interviews in general, are not so much a force for altering the course of politics as for accelerating it: speeding the formation of public attitudes and of the government response to them.

If the television interview is a means to the discovery of truth, its usefulness is limited. There have been few examples of men who have treated it with respect as such; and they have not been politicians. Perhaps it is no surprise that the one who comes to mind most readily is Edward R. Murrow, who once practised the form himself. As director of the United States Information Agency in the Kennedy administration he passed through London in January 1962 on his way to Paris. In the nissen hut which still served part of the airport at that time as a press conference room, he gave one or two broadcast interviews; mainly about Berlin, which was in the news at the time. Every two minutes a plane roared past a few hundred feet away as it took off. When it was my turn to put the questions, Mr Murrow paid grave and close attention to a beginner in a profession he had founded. In his replies he seemed to concentrate on answering the question as put and explaining what was in his own mind as clearly as he could. He made a deep impression: no one there had heard it done before. But Mr Murrow was only a politician by adoption.

7 Mighty Opposites

It is often said that political television tends to blur issues. If this means that television sometimes has difficulty in putting them into pictures, or in getting politicians to put them into words, it would seem to have force. But there is at least one form in which television regularly seeks to clarify or sharpen issues: the confrontation.

There is a good deal of excuse for the mistaken belief that just as a triangle has three sides, so – in the geometry of ideas – an issue has two: two and no more. The crude facts of political life support it: many of the laws and customs about fair play in broadcast argument support it: even the data of a television studio support it, where two disputants and a man in the middle make the most manageable scene. An old NBC radio programme, *Town Meeting of the Air,* used to begin with a ringing declaration that 'There are two sides to every question' before a gavel fell. It was inevitable that television should first adopt this view and then try whenever possible to clothe the two sides in flesh and blood.

The confrontation is the interview in a new dimension of reality. The buttons are off the foils. The difficulty about the relative standing of the two parties is removed. If the interview cannot match parliamentary dispute, bring both disputants into the studio.

A difficulty at the outset is that they are not always willing to come. Many politicians have strong reservations about the confrontation, and only think it useful in special cases. Since all great political parties are coalitions, some of the most crucial political arguments take place inside a single party. Few politicians are ready to be seen arguing publicly with fellow party members. More than one Labour MP has withdrawn from a television discussion, or been withdrawn by a political superior, because a figure from another wing of the party was to be there too.

A politician's style shows clearly in his attitude to confrontation. Adlai Stevenson had a horror of it. During his 1956 campaign for the presidency he refused to challenge President Eisenhower to a debate, because he thought the challenge would be taken as a gimmick. When Mr Stevenson later wrote an article advocating free television time for 'a great debate for the presidency', he said in the next sentence: 'I don't mean a debate in the literal collegiate sense of that word.'[1] As American ambassador to the United Nations during the Cuban crisis in October 1962, he found himself in a kind of courtroom confrontation with his Russian colleague. 'All right, sir, let me ask you a simple question: do you, Ambassador Zorin, deny that the USSR has placed and is placing medium- and intermediate-range missiles and sites in Cuba? Yes or no? Don't wait for the translation. Yes or no?' A great many Americans who saw it on television thought this Mr Stevenson's finest hour, and wrote to tell him so. He himself was a little ashamed of it afterwards. He thought he had only made it more difficult for the Russians to back down.[2]

Richard Nixon, on the other hand, who was twice on the presidential ticket that defeated Adlai Stevenson, relished the device – at least throughout the first phase of his career. In his 1960 campaign speeches he made extensive use of his argument with Nikita Khrushchev in the kitchen of a model home at the United States National Exhibition in Moscow in July 1959. (Nixon: 'I worked in my father's grocery.' Khrushchev: 'All shopkeepers are thieves.') His style of oratory conjured confrontations out of his past. 'So the Prime Minister said to me, "Mr Vice President, why is it..." And I said to him, "Mr Prime Minister..."'

The chief use of television confrontations has naturally been at election times, when the number of sides to an issue is commonly limited for the moment to two. Yet politicians have always known that there are dangers here. If broadcasting brought back in America the nineteenth-century debate between candidates, it was a hesitant return. As early as 1948 there was a radio debate in the Oregon Republican primary between Harold Stassen and Governor Thomas Dewey, who went on to lose to President Truman; but the example was not much taken up. It was not until 1956 that a presidential nomination was debated again, when Adlai Stevenson met Senator Estes Kefauver in a Miami television studio. Later they were both on the same defeated Democratic ticket. Broadcast debate began to look like a recourse for the unsuccessful.

Politicians had their scruples justified when they saw what happened to Richard Nixon in the most celebrated instance of all. In 1960 he broke the old, unspoken rule that a candidate in the lead stays aloof from his challenger. Share your platform with him, and you share your lead. Until then you may be the man in possession, the man on the inside: better informed, better placed, better known. But the debate comes, and your opponent is not struck by lightning. In fact, he appears to live in very much the same world: there he is sitting beside you. And he is now much better known.

Vice President Nixon decided that he would profit from a television debate with the junior senator from Massachusetts, John F. Kennedy, after watching him accept the Democratic presidential nomination in the Los Angeles Coliseum in July 1960.[3] Thirty-five million other Americans were watching too. The Vice President thought the Senator tired and maladroit. The debates were already being discussed between the parties: Mr Nixon presumably believed they would clinch his advantage as the more experienced, more reliable contender.

Senator Kennedy welcomed the debates because he believed they would dissipate this advantage. If he showed the greater foreknowledge, it was partly because he had had occasion to test the belief in the West Virginia primary in May: he was doing less well than Senator Humphrey before they appeared together in a Charleston television studio, and he made ground as a result. At the Los Angeles convention, again, he was generally considered to have given a more effective performance than Senator Lyndon Johnson of Texas in a televised encounter in front of the delegations of their two states.[4]

The four Kennedy-Nixon confrontations were more nearly debates than the seven between Lincoln and Douglas, but their shape was still formalised. They each filled an hour. In the first and fourth the candidates began with eight-minute speeches, answered ten questions antiphonally from a group of broadcasting reporters, and ended with speeches lasting about four minutes. In the two middle debates the argument was more nearly direct: in a programme that consisted entirely of answers to questions, the two candidates were allowed to comment on each other's answers. Answers were limited to two and a half minutes, comments to one and a half.[5]

Although more people believed Senator Kennedy to have come out on top than Mr Nixon, it is difficult to say that the Senator won. For that, he would have had to overwhelm the Vice President to the point where there was clearly no contest any more. But certainly Mr Nixon had not won either; and for him, as the man who ought to have won, that was tantamount to losing. He had set out to demonstrate the gap between him and his opponent: he had allowed it to be narrowed almost to nothing.

Despite this documenting of the perils of television debate, the device continued in use at slightly lower levels. During the mid-term elections in 1962 there were debates in the contests for governorships or senate seats in about a dozen states. In Ohio Senator Frank Lausche refused to debate with his Republican opponent, John Marshall Briley. Mr Briley thereupon prepared a programme, and got it shown on some Ohio stations, in which he presented the Senator's views on old film and his own opposing views from the studio. The Federal Communications Commission could not decide whether this was fair or not.[6] Senator Lausche held his seat easily anyway: he was unbeatable in polyglot Ohio at the time because he could cry in four languages.

To allow the 1960 presidential debates at all, it had been necessary for the two houses of Congress to agree on suspending section 315 of the Communications Act of 1934. The section demands equal broadcasting opportunities for all legally qualified candidates for the same public office, and in 1960 there were sixteen candidates for the presidency, counting the American Vegetarian Party and the Greenback Party and the rest. Section 315 was not suspended the next time. President Kennedy had said he would debate with his 1964 opponent: President Johnson in 1964 did not feel himself bound by the promise. Bills waiving section 315 again had been passed in both houses of Congress in 1963, and by May of 1964 a common version had been agreed upon. But somehow there was delay in both houses, and when the bill finally came up in the Senate in August it was killed – reportedly on the President's direct instructions.[7] The forms were complied with: even after the opportunity in law had disappeared, the President was still saying that he had reached no decision on debates with Senator Goldwater and Senator Goldwater was still asking his audiences 'Why won't the President debate with me?' He knew the answer: he had himself refused public discussion with Governor Rockefeller or Governor Scranton when they were his weaker rivals for the Republican nomination a month or two before.

*

By 1968, therefore, the principle that the man behind seeks confrontation and the man in front avoids it was well established.

Senator Robert Kennedy understood it well. He spent the last six weeks of his life, in the early summer of 1968, contesting four primaries against Senator Eugene McCarthy of Minnesota. He was expected to win them all; and he did win the first two, in Indiana and Nebraska. Throughout those two campaigns and the third, in Oregon, he ignored Senator McCarthy's repeated invitations to a debate. But he lost in Oregon. The morning after the votes were counted he flew south to California, where the fourth contest was to be, and said he would be glad to debate with Senator McCarthy at any time. A reporter at Los Angeles airport asked him why he only now agreed. 'Conditions', said Senator Kennedy with that half smile of self-knowledge which disarmed criticism, 'have changed.'

A single encounter was finally staged on a sunny June evening at KGO-TV, the American Broadcasting Company's affiliate station on Golden Gate Avenue in San Francisco. It was the last Saturday of the campaign. A small McCarthy crowd stood in the street chanting 'Gene in sixty-eight, Bobby will have to wait' as the candidates arrived. Inside Studio A, on a mezzanine floor, the two candidates sat down on the further side of a round table with the three ABC men who were to put pairs of questions to them. The white shirts which everyone was wearing, and the plain white cyclorama behind them, came out sky-blue even on the colour television sets in the building: an odd inversion from the early days of black-and-white television, when blue shirts came out white.

At the end of a campaign which had tended more and more towards acrimony, especially on the subject of television debates, the debate itself was chiefly remarkable for its uncontentiousness. Whether the point at issue was government money for negro areas or jet aircraft for Israel, the two candidates declared themselves in agreement. The time came when the three questioners, like Roman ringmasters whose beasts refused to fight, betrayed a certain irritation at the even tenor of the talk. With outstretched hand Senator Kennedy insistently explained: 'I have a great admiration for Senator McCarthy.'

Both men were playing down their differences; and this in itself showed the limited usefulness to which television confrontations between professional politicians had already been reduced. Senator Kennedy was partly aware that even if he won the California

Democratic primary he would still stand in need of Senator McCarthy's help to win the Democratic nomination. But more than that, the advice he had received was all in favour of a peaceable approach. His chief helper in the matter of the debate had been Pierre Salinger, once his elder brother's press secretary. In 1964, the year after President Kennedy's death, Mr Salinger had briefly been a senator from California: he was appointed to fill a vacancy. He lost the seat to a former Hollywood song-and-dance man, George Murphy; and the peak of that campaign was a television exchange in which Mr Salinger won all the points and yet was somehow left looking like an un-American bad guy who had roughed up the all-American good guy. Senator Kennedy will have been left in no doubt that attack was the best means to defeat.

Senator McCarthy, too, seemed reconciled to the fact that the encounter, like the whole succession of primaries, had become a contest in charm rather than in intellectual force. He was less reconciled than he looked. Although he accepted the view that he would not profit from attacking Senator Kennedy in public, he had nevertheless half hoped that ABC's three questioners would save him the trouble. 'There were several points', he said on CBS's *Face the Nation* the following morning, 'on which I didn't think they either raised the right points or that their follow-up was as hard as it should have been.' Chief of these points in his mind was a Kennedy advertisement repeatedly used in college newspapers which had unfairly represented Senator McCarthy's voting record on civil rights. Yet he had foreseen his own dissatisfaction. Two days before the debate he had said it was 'a kind of a charity programme for ABC, the way they're setting it up'.

ABC were not at the time financially or journalistically the most robust of the three major networks. The reason given in the Kennedy camp for assigning the debate to ABC had been that they were the first network to offer time for it. In fact both CBS and NBC had suggested a less rigid formula than ABC's, with only one journalist to hold the ring, which Senator Kennedy had not found acceptable. He may also have been aware that two of the three proposed ABC reporters inclined, in the view of their colleagues, to the Kennedy side.

Besides the three journalists round the studio table, and a handful more at the back of the studio to keep watch for the press as a whole, there were at least a hundred more reporters upstairs. We were divided between two fourth-floor studios, each with a monitor set in it, according to whether we habitually travelled in the Kennedy or the McCarthy retinue. But the dozen or so British correspondents, having no settled practice, had to choose which camp they preferred. Nearly all of them chose to be McCarthyites.

In the Kennedy room there was almost unbroken silence. From the McCarthy room there was occasional laughter as Senator Kennedy sounded over-familiar notes: references to his part in handling the Berlin and Cuba crises, reminders that he had been attorney-general, the ineluctable quotation from Camus. These were probably little noticed further afield. In general the whole hour was oddly levelling. Senator McCarthy's greater fastidiousness of thought and speech, Senator Kennedy's more intense disquiet over the condition of the poor in America, both seemed submerged in a shared anxiety to be affable. Victory was claimed for neither side, and there seemed no reason to suppose that the debate had much bearing on Senator Kennedy's narrow victory at the polls three days later.

There was one other televised encounter between presidential contenders before the substantive candidates were finally chosen. Vice President Humphrey, indisputably the man in front after Senator Kennedy's death, temporised on the question of a debate with Senator McCarthy until the week before the Democratic convention. Then he was able to turn it down 'in light of the sensitive international situation' after the Russian invasion of Czechoslovakia, and because two new candidates were trying to move in on the debate: Senator George McGovern of South Dakota and Governor Lester Maddox of Georgia. Senator McCarthy, knowing by then that he could not win the nomination, made no protest. But the obligations of conventioneering achieved what eight weeks of desultory negotiation had not been able to. The 174 delegate votes which Robert Kennedy had won in California were now floating free. At the convention Jesse Unruh, Speaker of the California Assembly and chairman of the state delegation, invited all the candidates except Governor Maddox (who was already thinking of going home) to meet the delegation at the same time on the morning before nomination day. He also invited the cameras. None of the guests could see any good reason to refuse.

So the Vice President and the two senators ascended to the ornate ballroom on the nineteenth floor of the LaSalle Hotel in Chicago to take turns at making a couple of brief speeches, answering a couple of questions, and commenting on each other's answers. Perhaps it was the shared background of the three men in upper-midwestern academic life that gave the occasion a cosy and yet literate quality. If the electorate at large had been choosing between the three men they would have found the exchanges helpful. But by now the electorate was 2622 convention delegates. Most of them will have watched the debate on television; but their votes turned on other considerations.

By any immediate test the winner was Senator McGovern. As the latecomer to the contest, he combined exactly the right degrees of humility, jocularity and Methodist pulpit earnestness. Several times the Californian delegates stood up to clap him. Senator McCarthy, on the other hand, was elegantly and evidently bored; and Mr Humphrey could only offer the flaccid phrases he had wrapped himself in for years. 'I can stand before this audience and not only claim a record, as my colleagues can, but also claim a vision and a dream.' The vision still had the Vietnam war in it, and the dream amounted to nothing much more than keeping Mr Nixon out of the White House. Yet when all the delegates were counted the next night, Mr Humphrey's name led all the rest, and Senator McGovern was a bad third.

Efforts to bring a televised debate into the substantive post-convention campaign had begun long before. By October 1967 five bills for suspending section 315 of the Communications Act were before the Senate Communications Subcommittee. The subcommittee chairman was Senator John Pastore of Rhode Island, the man who had proclaimed at the 1964 Democratic convention that 'God did bless America on that day four years ago in Los Angeles when John F. Kennedy said "I need you, Lyndon Johnson"'; so that for as long as President Johnson was the putative Democratic candidate, action against his wishes was unlikely.

After Mr Johnson withdrew his name in March 1968 the networks renewed their persuasions that section 315 should be lifted, and through the summer and early autumn appropriate measures made progress at a snail's pace through both houses of Congress. But now the only candidate with his hand up in favour of debate was Mr Humphrey, who found himself in a new struggle where he was no longer favoured to win; and Mr Nixon could point to the presence of a third major candidate, Mr Wallace, as a reason why the scheme – attractive though it was – would be difficult of execution. His friends in Congress took the point. Mr Nixon's private attitude on this as on other things was less subtly expressed by his vice-presidential candidate, Governor Agnew of Maryland, who was a little slow to realise that there are some things in politics which need not be said in so many words. In Casper, Wyoming, in mid-September the Governor said he doubted whether Mr Nixon would ever agree to a debate: 'It's poor tactics when you're running so far ahead.'

In Britain there was no general election for four years after the 1960 presidential election in America. British politicians had four years to digest the lessons of the Kennedy-Nixon debates. They digested them thoroughly. In the 1964 election, at the national level, there were no confrontations at all: in 1966 only between a few party spokesmen. The dominant figure in both elections was Harold Wilson. In both his line was to be ready in public for debates with his opponent, and to hold off in private.

In 1964 the Labour party pressed for single combat between their man and Sir Alec Douglas-Home. The Tories, preferring to trust in the overall worth of their front bench ('we bat all the way down to number eleven'), proposed a group of encounters between the senior figures on each side: not so much *Sohrab and Rustum* as *The Fair Maid of Perth*. Mr Wilson's reluctance seems to have had a number of layers. His ostensible reason for frowning on the idea was that to pit his shadow foreign secretary against the Conservatives' real one was unconstitutional and unwise: he did not yet know who his real foreign secretary would be. (In fact after the election he filled nearly all his senior posts from the men who had been covering the same field in opposition.) More realistically, he was apprehensive about how some of his colleagues might perform. Beyond that he was not incontrovertibly sure that he could himself pulverise Sir Alec;[8] and then there was the question of whether pulverisation would be electorally useful. To demonstrate that one's opponent was an amateur might have an unintended effect in a country of devoted amateurs.

In the election just under eighteen months later the objection to Labour frontbenchers as debaters could be lifted without much risk: Labour's theme in the campaign was after all 'you *know* Labour government works'. But by now the Prime Minister had even less incentive to a personal debate. He was the man in front. The

Conservatives were none too eager either, with a new leader whom they were still uncertain about long after the election. The question might not have come up at all if it had not been for the accidents of television interviewing. At the end of February 1966 Alastair Burnet, interviewing the Conservative leader for ITV, found that Edward Heath's terse style of answering had run through all the pointful questions before the time was up. The gap was filled with a question about willingness to debate, Mr Heath could only say he was in favour, and the issue was in the open.

The discussions were long and complicated; but basically the blocking tactic which the Prime Minister used was a very simple one. He compelled the Conservative leader to share in his own reluctance by insisting that the Liberal leader, Jo Grimond, should appear with them. Mr Heath rejected this as a 'tea party', and he had no other choice: he would have been dividing his eminence with a lesser competitor just as surely as the Prime Minister would have been. So there were no confrontations between party leaders.

Whether television confrontation helps a wise choice between candidates is open to dispute. There is now no telling whether Henry Steele Commager was right that 'Washington would have lost a television debate'.[9] Lincoln did lose his series of debates, in that he failed to win the senate seat at issue; but they helped him to the presidency two years later. Not many viewers detected in John F. Kennedy's debating performance the qualities for which he was afterwards admired: yet it was the debates more than any other one thing which helped him defeat Richard Nixon.

The purpose of confrontation is to make clearer the differences between candidates' opinions. Since the differences that need clarification are mostly ones of detail, this is a tall order for the spoken word in conditions where candidates and viewers have so many other things in their head at the same time: appearance, amiability, political advantage. Clarification has not been a common result of television debate. The main conclusion drawn from a study of thirty-one research projects on the Kennedy-Nixon debates was the unsurprising one that the viewers 'discovered how well each candidate could perform in a debate'.[10] That was all: not how they would choose between different courses of action with more than a few seconds to decide.

Since candidates for the job of British prime minister have never taken part in a television debate, there can be no certainty whether the device would be more useful in Britain. It might well be less useful. The most boring and destructive tendency in British politics is the urge among politicians to blame all trouble on the other side. The tendency may proceed from an accurate reading of what their voters want. There is evidence that most viewers enjoy argument.[11] Although fewer enjoy polemic, there is always a body of believers who look forward to catching the spokesman for the other side with egg, if not blood, on his face. But television is not necessarily serving a sound purpose if it satisfies that craving.

Among American politicians, as the 1968 campaign showed, there is a more general belief that voters do not relish sharp argument, especially between presidential candidates and especially on television. But this belief has only led to the intellectual bowdlerisation of television debate. Hard sayings of all kinds must be excluded.

With so many perils and restraints involved, then, it is no great loss that the cautiousness of successful politicians has made high-level television debate a comparative rarity.

8   The Way to Downing Street

On the morning of Sir Winston Churchill's ninetieth birthday in November 1964, less than two months before his death, he said a dozen kindly words to an ITN reporter who approached him with a microphone outside his house in Hyde Park Gate. With that marginal exception, he never gave an interview or a talk specifically for television.

He was the last leader of any British political party of whom that was true. He had resigned the Conservative leadership in April 1955. After that time television cameras became a familiar sight in Downing Street, and a familiar instrument for rival party leaders aspiring to the same address. Within five years in the middle sixties, all three significant British parties had a change of leadership: Labour and the Conservatives in 1963, the Conservatives again in 1965, the Liberals in 1967. By then all three of the new leaders had spent the greater part if not all of their political life in the era of television. They knew what could be expected from it and how they were expected to treat it. When Harold Wilson arrived at Transport House one evening in February 1963 as the new leader of the Labour party, there was a live camera from ITV in the tiny hallway. As the reporter harnessed to it I rose in his path with a microphone and congratulations. Even then, Mr Wilson knew exactly what to do. He accepted the congratulations, but declined comment: 'I have to say something inside first.' Party leadership would never be without these accompaniments again. By the time Edward Heath and Jeremy Thorpe came to it, the pattern was set: a party leader's first evening in office was not to be spent in celebrating with his family, or even in comforting his disappointed colleagues, but in sprinting round London to appear in as many television programmes as possible.

These men had been chosen for their performance not on television but in the House of Commons. Yet television played some part either in the way they came to power or in the way they kept it.

*

The parliamentary Labour party chose Harold Wilson as their leader on the calculation, supported by his showing during the leadership struggle itself, that he was by far their best Commons debater. The calculation proved right. What did not enter into their judgments was the fact that for some time to come he would also be their best television performer. They had had almost no evidence of it. Until he began to consolidate the party's strength and his own position with a series of tactful television appearances, he had never shown his television form.

George Brown, the man he defeated in the final round, had not shown his either. There had been an interesting hint of it, though, a week before the first round of voting in the leadership election. The British government's first prolonged effort to get into the European communities had just come to nothing, and as prime minister Harold Macmillan made a television broadcast about it which was carried by the BBC and ITV. George Brown, as acting leader of the Labour party since Hugh Gaitskell's death twelve days before, held that the broadcast had partisan implications and asked to be allowed to reply to it. The BBC said no, and were not pressed. ITV said yes, and then tried to rescind the invitation. Mr Brown made a successful protest and a successful broadcast; but the protest involved some undiplomatic exchanges with the Independent Television Authority which came at a bad time for him.

Examples of Mr Brown's volatility were not confined to television and his dealings with it; but more than one of them occurred on television, including the one that may have done him the most harm: his broadcast in November 1963 on the evening of President Kennedy's death. He had been fetched to an ITV studio from a well-furnished municipal dinner-table in east London, and he spoke of the dead president with unquestioned grief but with a warmth which embarrassed several Labour MPs. The fuss which the affair gave rise to may have been disproportionate, but it contributed to a feeling even among MPs who had voted for him nine months earlier that he could not now be considered as a potential prime minister.[1]

This did not seem important at the time, when Mr Wilson was entrenched; but it became important when the second Wilson government met economic trouble. In July 1966 Mr Brown was head of the Department of Economic Affairs, and still an advocate of the government's original policy of economic expansion, when the third sterling crisis in two years enforced a sharp deflation. Mr Brown thought a sterling devaluation would have been preferable: he acknowledged as much after he had left the government altogether;[2] and when television news cameras filmed him stalking into 10 Downing Street on that July evening, it had already been made known by ITN that he had written a letter of resignation. But a resignation at that level would have done nothing for foreign confidence in the new measures, and television viewers were next regaled with a midnight recantation on the steps of Number Ten. Mr Brown was to stay in the government. Three weeks later it was learned that he was to take over the Foreign Office.

It was the climactic incident of his life. It brought him twenty months in a job he had always wanted: yet both the fact of it and the manner of it made sure that he would never reach the job he had wanted even more, the premiership. The government did devalue sterling sixteen months later. After opposing the step for three years, Mr Wilson was able to stay in office partly because of the manifest unavailability of any immediate replacement. It is at least arguable that if Mr Brown, as an advocate of earlier devaluation, had incurred less criticism on personal grounds, he might have been that replacement. In significant instances the grounds for criticism either arose or were first aired on television. To that limited extent television may have influenced the choice of a British party leader.

A similarly negative example is provided by the career of Sir Alec Douglas-Home. Although it was on a BBC television interview during the Conservative conference at Blackpool in October 1963 that he first made his interest in the Conservative succession apparent, it was not television which brought Sir Alec to power a few days later. His television exposure until that time had been almost entirely limited to curt airport interviews as foreign secretary. Nor was his television showing a prime factor in his leaving the Conservative leadership twenty-one months later. The immediate cause of his decision to resign, a newspaper article by William Rees-Mogg which likened Sir Alec to a prewar county cricket captain who compiled a small but useful score at an awkward moment 'when the wicket was taking spin at Canterbury or Weston-super-Mare', made no mention of television.[3]

The fact remains that Sir Alec might have stayed in the job a great deal longer if it had not been for television. He was not a disaster on television; but he was not enough of a success.

He had his successes. In his first interview after he became prime minister he was asked about Labour attacks on him as the fourteenth earl – a dignity he was on the point of laying aside in order to get back into the Commons. He said he supposed Mr Wilson was really, when you came to think of it, the fourteenth Mr Wilson. In the simple coin of political repartee this was considered golden. Furthermore, during his time of trial, the 1964 election, he was handled by television people with great care and even generosity. His face (as would doubtless be true of many other people who never have occasion to discover it) looked odd from several angles. Cameramen went to great lengths to avoid unflattering shots. They were spurred on by an incident early in the campaign in the market square at Norwich when an ITN crew, trapped by the crowd at one side of the speakers' platform, could only film an extreme profile shot which drew anguished cries from Conservative Central Office. Filmed interviews for news purposes seldom call for make-up; but the BBC at one stage made a rule that Sir Alec was always to be made up for interviews. (This meant, if the occasion was a shared one with ITN, that an ITN interviewer sitting knee-to-knee with Sir Alec and on the point of asking his first question suddenly found it necessary to make conversation instead while a girl in a pink smock went to work with a set of small sponges.) As a public speaker, Sir Alec was prone to fluffs or verbal slips: television editors only included them in what was publicly screened when there was no avoiding them. Enormous care was lavished by an ITV company on the production for both networks of his final message.[4]

In spite of all this, the viewers were not won round. The statistical evidence is clear. In the third week before polling, National Opinion Polls asked confessed viewers of political television which of the three party leaders they found most impressive on television. Even among the Conservative-inclined, less than half gave Sir Alec's name.[5] BBC Audience Research looked into the reaction to their three 'Election Forums', in each of which one party leader was asked questions adapted from ones sent in on postcards. The programmes went out on radio at the same time as on television, so that the reaction here was not simply to party leaders in vision. But on the basis of reports from 'standing panels of ordinary viewers and listeners', BBC Audience Research concluded that 'Labour supporters were better pleased with their leader's performance than Conservative supporters were with theirs. In the judgment of not only anti-Conservatives but also of the Uncommitted, the answers given by Sir Alec were a good deal less satisfactory than those given by either Mr Grimond or Mr Wilson.'⁶

There were undoubtedly other reasons why Sir Alec gave up the Conservative leadership, and why his colleagues did not beg him too insistently to hold on to it. In the Commons itself he was not an inspiring leader of the opposition. Yet he was not the first or the last to meet that difficulty, and he might very well have survived it. Edward Heath had his troubles with the job from the outset. As his first speech as leader of the opposition wound on, Archie Manuel could be heard to call across from the other side of the House in the grating accents of Central Ayrshire: 'Let's have Alec back!'

But in the summer of 1965, with Labour's overall majority in the Commons down to three, the Conservatives knew that they might have to face an election at any time. If they were to have any hope of winning it, they would need a leader who could attack Harold Wilson effectively and from a basis of equal competence. It would be on television that this attack would be chiefly seen and judged. It does therefore seem fair to conclude that television was at least a persuasion in Sir Alec's going.

The story had a happy ending: Sir Alec's repute in the party was unshakable ever after. There was almost no precedent for voluntary retirement from that job, and his followers were duly grateful.

Sir Alec had a talent for happy endings achieved too late. His equability appeared to best advantage, in the tradition of the British upper class, in the moment of departure or defeat. It was his brother William Douglas-Home, the playwright, who first drew attention to this. He once disclosed that he got the idea for *The Chiltern Hundreds*, in which the family butler stands for Parliament in the Conservative interest, from the fact that when his elder brother – then called Lord Dunglass – lost his seat at Lanark in the 1945 election, the only member of the household who seemed at all disturbed was the butler.

Just after he had resigned as Prime Minister at Buckingham Palace, Sir Alec gave a television interview at Conservative Central Office. He was asked about Mr Khrushchev's removal from office the day before. 'Clearly Mr Khrushchev has been deposed and did not retire. I wish he hadn't been deposed at all. I wish,' he added with a broad and totally unresentful smile, 'I hadn't been deposed.'

If television was important in the departure of Sir Alec, it was not so important in the choice of his successor. Effectively there were only two contenders, Edward Heath and Reginald Maudling. Enoch Powell's candidacy at that time was formal. The choice was to be made by a secret ballot of all Conservative MPs. Considering that the Conservatives had never used anything like this system before, the process was astonishingly placid and orderly. Tory MPs stood in line to vote in Committee Room 14 of the House of Commons as if it were all the greatest fun in the world. Except for a few enemies that Mr Heath had made as chief whip or as the minister responsible for ending resale price maintenance early in 1964, no one seemed to feel that either candidate would be anything but a success in Parliament or in the country.

To judge from comments at the time, television prowess was scarcely a factor. It was taken as read that both men could manage very well. Because he was considered to have done well on television during the Brussels negotiations in 1962-3, Mr Heath had been chosen as front man for party broadcasts during the 1964 election: on the other hand, Mr Maudling had been much praised during the same campaign for his handling of party press conferences, which involved constant television interviews.

If any extra-parliamentary factor intruded, it may have been the reported word that 'the City is for Ted' – including some very influential parts of the City. But what chiefly worked for Mr Heath was his parliamentary success that summer in leading an effective opposition to the government's complicated Finance Bill. The new voting system for the leadership allowed three ballots: Mr Heath put a decent distance between himself and his two competitors on the first one, they both retired, and it was all over.

Whether or not the leadership of the modern Liberal party is considered a likely resting-place on the way to Downing Street, it is worth recording that the motives in that choice too have remained chiefly parliamentary. When Jo Grimond resigned in January 1967, Jeremy Thorpe was chosen by his colleagues in the Commons not as his party's most accomplished remaining broadcaster, although he had wide experience on radio at least, but as their most accomplished parliamentarian.

By 1968, therefore, television's record in British party leadership was no more than that it had been partly instrumental in causing one demotion and perhaps in preventing one promotion.

Television has had the same doubtful bearing on the behaviour of party leaders once appointed. It has not altered any politician's character; but it has sometimes represented character inaccurately and sometimes influenced a politician's style.

There has been a notion since television began that it is an un-faltering judge of character: that like some moral X-ray the camera bores into the heart of a man, peeling away the wrappers of in-sincerity and pretence. The belief persists even in America, where millions of viewers found they had been deceived for years in the late fifties by the agonisings of quiz-show contestants who knew the answers all the time. In Britain the theory has not been so brutally demolished; but anyone who has worked in television there, let alone political television, knows that characters regularly come out a little different on the screen.

More surprisingly, the misrepresentation is nearly always for the worse. It is an odd limitation in television that it has difficulty in rendering charm. There have been examples of television pro-fessionals who distilled more charm over the air than they possessed in person; but they have been few and transient. Much more com-mon in television is the figure whose engagingness deserts him the moment the camera is switched on. And this is particularly true of politicians.

Charm is not the first quality that anybody associates with poli-ticians. Their profession calls for too much self-assertiveness to leave room for a lot of it. Yet members of the staff of virtually every senior politician in Britain and America have been repeatedly heard to say, 'If only more people could see him when he's in a small group . . .' And in many cases they are right: citizens who only knew their leaders from television, and disliked them, might often find that a personal encounter changed their minds. The close contact that television seems to provide between viewer and viewed is partly illusory. Television seldom transmits a man's private self: for the most part it transmits a public self in a private setting.

Politicians who suffer from this have themselves to blame in great measure. They insist on believing that only their public self is pre-sentable. Consciously or not, they apprehend the untruth of the idea that the camera cannot lie; but the lies they then feed it are the wrong ones. They are so anxious to suppress any evidence of ignorance or irresponsibility that they throw out their saving graces at the same time. In particular they betray very little sign of the scepticism which most of them feel about their own likely achievements and powers as politicians. They dare not confess fallibility.

In the mid-sixties, a man regularly hailed as the most attractive figure in British politics was Jo Grimond; and this quality remained with him on television. Its ground was that – at any rate as far as a political reporter had opportunity to judge – he was at less pains than other politicians to draw a line between his public and private characters. In the House of Commons, on an assembly platform, in a television studio, he would talk as one could imagine him talking at breakfast, except perhaps rather louder. (A television programme did once show him at breakfast.) He seemed prepared to acknowledge in so many words what no one else would, that there were parts of his profession which were absurd and parts which were hopeless. He knew when politics ought not to be taken seriously. It may have been a natural and even a necessary attitude in the leader of a party whose strength in the Commons never rose above a dozen; but it could usefully have been borrowed from time to time by other party leaders, and it never was.

It may be comforting to those who fear television demagogy that towards the end of the sixties there had still appeared no senior British politician who was appreciably more engaging on television, either as a person or as a merchant of ideas, than he was face to face. But it was a pity that the general effect of television was the other way: to represent most politicians as duller and less engaging than they were in fact.

From the moment Edward Heath became Conservative leader, he was beset with advice about how to behave on television; and being a professional, he was disposed to take it. But there was so much of it that if he had taken it all he would never have been able to open his mouth; particularly since the common element was that he should start by effacing his own character.

His natural instinct was to regard a television interview as war between him and the interviewer. In the autumn of 1962 an ITN crew was sent to meet him at Heathrow on one of his many returns from Common Market negotiations in Brussels. It was a routine encounter: the airport conference room was almost empty. When the interview began I asked him – there may have been something in the news which made it pointful – whether the Americans were trying to push us into the Common Market. No reply. Instead the Lord Privy Seal's tan deepened for about ten seconds before he asked me whether I would mind starting again. I said of course not, and I hadn't meant the question to be an awkward one, and I could easily think of something else. No, he said, ask me that one again. Was he sure? Quite sure. I asked the question again. With quiet satisfaction he produced the response he had determined on. 'No,' he said.

My turn to be discomfited, since only the best interviewers have follow-up questions ready for all emergencies. After another pause I produced some sort of supplementary question, and the interview took its normal course. But the chief interest of the occasion was that it was he who remembered it better than I did: he reminded me of it, not without pleasure in the recollection, four years later.

Conservative Central Office will have been unaware of the incident, but they were aware of the style, and when he became party leader they were anxious to bounce him out of it: the target was the viewer, not the interviewer. He was successfully coached to produce answers varying in length from a sentence to a paragraph, and to treat questions as pegs for his own discourse rather than as lances to be knocked aside; but it was some time before he gave the impression of being his own man on television. As late as October 1967 a reporter for *The Times* could describe him as showing 'an *unaccustomed* toughness and polish' in a BBC television interview after the party conference.[7]

Perhaps it is the British voter who creates these difficulties for the British politician. The British notoriously distrust intellect in their politicians. Some of their ablest leaders have thought it wise to seem a little less able than they were. When the British discuss politicians, the virtue they set the greatest store by is sincerity; which must mean, if it means anything at all, that they think it more important for a politician to believe in what he proposes than for the proposal itself to be wise. As a man who relished the intellectual more than the personal problems of politics, Mr Heath could not help occasionally disappointing an audience that felt in this way.

One of his best moments on television came when he appeared to make a conscious decision not to tell his audience what they wanted to hear. It was in his last broadcast of the 1966 campaign. All the indications were that his party was already beaten. He seemed to accept this himself; and he seemed almost to welcome it as a chance to say what interested him, in the full knowledge that it did not interest much of the electorate. 'There is a role for Britain to play which will take all we can give it for the rest of the century. That role is Europe. I want young people to be able to build in marble when my generation can only build in brick. I want them to see a strong economy and a united Europe as a starting point for their lives and ambitions.'[8] Electorally it had little pulling power; but a refusal to compromise is always impressive. It was Disraeli's 'the time will come when you will hear me' more gently expressed.

It would be impossible to discuss television's record in rendering the character of politicians without considering Harold Wilson. Even before he became Prime Minister in October 1964, he was widely looked on as the first complete television statesman – 'armed at point, exactly, cap-à-pie' to meet anything that television could throw at him and take advantage of it. Yet his own circle were well aware that however successful the television picture, it was not exactly their man that the viewers saw.

The Wilson use of television seemed at one time to challenge the constitution itself. There was a period, after his premiership had been confirmed by the 1966 election, when television was his power base in a more real sense than the House of Commons was. This was the meaning of his intermittent and semi-public threats to his dissident backbenchers. He was reminding them that through television he could appeal over their heads to the electorate. In name his strength was the majority which their election in their several constituencies had given him. In fact the Labour party's campaign had been largely fought under his banner, and it was fair to suppose that many voters in the seats Labour had won had been voting to keep the Prime Minister in office rather than to get a new member for Lancaster or Croydon South. The other side of this was that a number of these new members could not have won, and could not win again, without the Prime Minister's blessing. But he could withdraw it. At the time he controlled the party machinery, whatever the textbooks said: he could see to it that in almost every case the dissident would find party funds, party backing and the support of the local party faithful transferred to another candidate. The deterrent was only useful as long as it was never used, and as long as the opinion polls showed the Prime Minister to be widely admired. When that admiration flagged, some other mortar was needed for party unity in the Commons.

During the periods when Harold Wilson found favour with the electorate, his medium for finding it was television. He set a new standard for party leaders. There had been a time when they only needed to understand foreign affairs. Then they had to take in home affairs too. After the first Wilson election they had to be masters of television as well.

Like any good professional, he understood the given facts of the medium, technical and editorial, and was prepared to work within them. If a cameraman asked him to walk down the garden steps from the cabinet room, cross the lawn and stop on a certain leaf facing in a certain direction, he did it, without any sense of condescension, and got it right the first time. If it fell to him to begin some brief filming session by reading aloud the communiqué he was to answer questions about, he knew that he had to wait while the cameras were run up to speed before he spoke. He knew it was an editorial requirement that his news broadcasts should be ostensibly addressed to a questioner and not to the world at large. He never tried, as some politicians did, to steal a look at the camera when he wanted to emphasise a point. He realised that the effect would be slightly disquieting, like an actor stepping outside his part in the theatre, and that it would probably be cut out anyway.

In the experience of people who interviewed him regularly he very seldom tried to control what questions he was asked. He was content with an indication of the subjects. He knew what they would be anyway, and what he was prepared to say on each. He then simply listened for the key phrase in each question – east of Suez, or sterling, or opinion polls – and said what he had to say. By this method even the fiercest questioners were converted into an adjunct. They became human memorandum-pads: they presented the heads of the discourse.

His understanding of the character of journalists sometimes showed a touch too clearly, though not as a rule on television. He knew that the way to flatter newspapermen was to quote to them what they had written. With television interviewers this was more difficult, since they wrote virtually nothing; but he found a way.

At the end of his first visit to Paris as Prime Minister, in April

1965, he gave a press conference in a great gilt chamber near the Elysée Palace. It was chiefly for the French press. The issue that day, as not seldom since, was sterling; but since the French journalists there seemed unaware of it, and our film had to catch a plane in a hurry if it was to be shown in London that night, I jumped up and made some question about sterling heard. The Prime Minister seized on it with evident gratitude and delivered a trenchant answer in which he said that people who speculated against the pound (in the belief that it might be devalued) were 'nut-cases'. It had its effect on the exchanges. The next time he saw me he said, 'You know, you put five points on sterling with that question of yours.'

Very little of this appeared on television. When the camera was switched on and the interviewer began his first question, the Prime Minister's face was composed to a courteous attentiveness that was hardly deserved; but that was all. If he liked to demonstrate that he knew a reporter's name, so do all politicians; and he only did it with good reason. In January 1966 he flew to Lagos for the first Commonwealth prime ministers' conference to be held away from London. The atmosphere on the tarmac at Lagos airport was like the air inside the palm house at Kew. The Prime Minister was led to the VIP Lounge, a room about fifteen feet square without air conditioning. Inside it about a hundred journalists were waiting: mostly African, but with ITN and the BBC wedged at the front. The main problem was the Nigerian Ministry of Information. When the questioning finally started one of their officials, bearded and bespectacled, was still loudly organising us all. In the middle of an answer the Prime Minister broke off and said to him, pleasantly but firmly: 'Belt up, do you mind? I'm trying to answer a question from Mr Whale here.'

It was a political utterance of some skill. It made a number of points: that he knew the vernacular; that his liberalism was of the unforced kind which allowed him to speak to a black man with the kind of friendly rebuke only used among equals: that at the same time it did not extend to the point of allowing him to be publicly interrupted by a black man; and that with all this his real attention was reserved for his countrymen, his own, whom he knew by name.

A few days later the same official had his revenge when he came on the ITN cameraman taking forbidden pictures of soldiers, and had us surrounded with bayonets while he confiscated the camera.

But we got it back without having to complain to Downing Street.

In one respect it was a rare incident: it had in it an indication of flippancy which the Prime Minister rarely allowed himself on television. Television was for setting out the problem, a due concern about the problem, and the measures proposed to meet the problem. It was not for any expressions of self-doubt or deprecation. There was no place on television, therefore, for the private and pleasing Wilson axiom that Canute would have got different results at high tide – in other words that the moment to demonstrate your mastery of events was the moment when they were turning in your favour anyway. Perhaps it was as well not to publicise it: several people thought it was the principle on which the Prime Minister took overall responsibility for the country's economy in the summer of 1967. A few months later came the November devaluation; and six months after that the responsibility was quietly abandoned.

During those months Mr Wilson observed an unprecedented broadcast silence. His understanding of television extended to the realisation that television alone could not restore his damaged credit.

One reason why the television demagogue is still a far-off figure in British politics is that British politicians still have to establish themselves first in places that have nothing to do with television: the House of Commons, the department, the cabinet room. It is interesting, as a confirmatory footnote, to see how little success has been had in politics by people who established themselves first in television.

Even radio has a better record. Vernon Bartlett was said by A. J. P. Taylor to have won a by-election at Bridgwater in 1938 'solely on the strength of his talks on the radio'.[9] Dr Charles Hill rose from having been the BBC's Radio Doctor during the Second World War to cabinet rank and a peerage with the Conservatives in the early sixties – and then returned to his earlier profession as chairman successively of the ITA and the BBC. Douglas Houghton, a cabinet member in the first Wilson government and the early part of the second, had for years been a sort of radio tax doctor on a programme called *Can I Help You?* Both men were helped into Parliament in the first place by their radio repute.

Television, on the other hand, had done little more for the man-power of Parliament than to swell the ranks of unsuccessful Liberal candidates. Its brightest success was Christopher Chataway, an ITN newscaster of the fifties who became a junior education minister in the sixties for two years before the Conservatives went out of office.

In America, about the most notable prize to have fallen to an established television professional by 1966 was the governorship of the state of Oregon. In that year it was won for the Republicans by Tom McCall, who had been the state's leading television news commentator for eight years. Edward R. Murrow declined a possible Democratic senatorial nomination for the state of New York in 1958 and Eric Sevareid, another CBS man, one for North Dakota in 1967. But the question of the influence of television on the choosing of political leaders is very much more complex in America than it is in Britain.

9 Television Studio to White House

Television has been a much more deliberately used force in bringing forward candidates for the American presidency, and indeed for all high political office in America, than for the British premiership. There have been two main reasons for this: one historical, one legal. As a matter of history, American politicians have regularly detected the power of television in politics at several levels. As a matter of law, there is very much less restraint on the political use of television in America than in Britain. For all practical purposes, American politicians can have as much of it as they can afford.

By the end of 1960, politically interested Americans had already twice been fascinated by instances of the effect that television could apparently have on the careers of individual politicians.

The first instance was in the fall of Joseph McCarthy. Senator McCarthy's period of power began one afternoon in February 1950 when he held up a piece of paper in front of the Ohio County Women's Republican Club at Wheeling, West Virginia, and said: 'I have here in my hand a list of two hundred and five that were known to the Secretary of State as being members of the Communist Party and who nevertheless are still working and shaping the policy of the State Department.'[1] Formally speaking, the Senator's influence ended in December 1954 when his colleagues voted three to one to condemn him for bringing the Senate into dishonour and disrepute. In fact it had ended six months before, in the senate caucus room, during hearings into charges and counter-charges between Senator McCarthy and the United States Army, when counsel for the Army protested before the television cameras against a move of the Senator's.

The army counsel, Joseph Welch, came from a Boston law firm which also employed a young lawyer who as a student had been a member of the National Lawyers' Guild. At the time of the hearings the Guild was believed to be under Communist control. For his own professional protection the man had not been allowed to work on the case. Seven weeks after the beginning of the hearings the Senator suddenly brought up his name as a weapon against the army presentation.

Roy Cohn, who had been counsel to the Investigations Sub-committee under Senator McCarthy's chairmanship and was still his chief assistant now that the Senator appeared before it, has since said that he had made a compact with the army counsel not to let the matter come up; and that the Senator had approved it.[2] Whether or not Mr Welch felt an added sense of shock because of this, it drew from him – a sixty-three-year-old New England lawyer in a floppy bow tie – a long-remembered tirade beginning: 'Until this moment, Senator, I think I never really gauged your cruelty or your recklessness'; and ending: 'I like to think that I am a gentle man, but your forgiveness will have to come from someone other than me.' The Senator interposed an objection. Mr Welch answered it and said: 'Let us not assassinate this lad further, Senator. You have done enough. Have you no sense of decency, sir? At long last? Have you left no sense of decency?'

Against all the rules, he was applauded as he closed the discussion.[3]

The 35 days of the hearings produced 187 hours of television; and this at a period when television was still watched in a darkened room, more or less without competitors for attention. At the time of the Wheeling speech in 1950 there had been about four million television sets in use in the United States: at the time of the hearings four years later there were over 27 million. 1954 itself was the year of the television industry's greatest growth. At the end of June 1953 there were 199 television stations on the air across the country: a year later there were 408.[4] Probably a third of the adults in the country watched Senator McCarthy in action during the hearings; and many of them were seeing him for the first time. After the hearings his senate colleagues felt brave enough to move against him.

The other episode which persuaded American politicians that a new force had come among them was an ascent, not a decline: the transformation of John F. Kennedy from a losing to a winning candidate after his televised debates with Richard Nixon. A survey done for CBS suggested that 57 per cent of those who voted in the 1960 presidential election believed that the debates had influenced their decisions. Out of nearly 69 million votes cast, the Kennedy margin on the popular vote was about 113,000.[5]

These were the two cases which were held particularly striking; but there were several other examples among senior politicians of careers which appeared to have been advanced, upheld or retarded on television.

Richard Nixon himself salvaged his vice-presidential candidacy in September 1952 with a television appearance which many people believe he never bettered, in his own terms. There had been trouble about a supplement to his senate salary subscribed by wealthy constituents in California. With his wife beside him, he went on television from Los Angeles to set out his financial affairs. At the end he said his wife had no mink coat – though 'I always tell her that she'd look good in anything' – and confessed that they had recently accepted a gift from a well-wisher. 'You know what it was? It was a little cocker spaniel dog in a crate that he sent all the way from Texas. Black and white spotted. And our little girl – Tricia, the six-year-old – named it Checkers. And you know the kids love that dog and I just want to say this right now, that regardless of what they say about it, we're going to keep it . . .'

As a mark of the Nixons' real debt to that dog the occasion became known as the Checkers broadcast. At least a million people responded to it with messages of support; and it drew from General Eisenhower, when the two men next met – also, oddly enough, at Wheeling, West Virginia – one of the few expressions of regard for his running-mate he was ever heard to offer: 'You're my boy, Dick.' The Nixon candidacy continued.[6]

Another contender in that same campaign year might not have been there but for television. Senator Estes Kefauver of Tennessee let the cameras in to his itinerant hearings when he was chairman of the Senate's Special Committee to Investigate Organised Crime in Interstate Commerce. In March 1951 the fidgeting hands of an underworld prince named Frank Costello – his lawyer had kept the cameras off his face – became one of the first national television spectacles.[7] By January 1952 the Senator was well enough known to declare for the Democratic presidential nomination.

Governor Adlai Stevenson, who defeated Senator Kefauver for that nomination, profited from television to become known outside Illinois. Robert Kennedy became a new and more appealing Kefauver between 1954 and 1959 as counsel to another series of televised senate investigations.[8] When Henry Cabot Lodge won the New Hampshire Republican primary in March 1964 without leaving his job as ambassador in Saigon, the chief means used on his behalf was an old five-minute film made for his vice-presidential effort in 1960, with a sound-track lifted from an even older after-dinner speech of President Eisenhower's. It was shown 39 times in three weeks by the only commercial television station in New Hampshire. The man who made the original film was in no doubt that Mr Lodge would never have seemed such an attractive candidate if he had shown himself to the voters of New Hampshire in person.[9]

In June of the same year Governor William Scranton of Pennsylvania forfeited on CBS's *Face the Nation* what chance he had of winning the Republican presidential nomination. He had intended to read on the air his declaration that he was a candidate. Instead he could only give an accurate picture of his own confusion after General Eisenhower had seemingly given and then withheld support. It was then that Mr Scranton began to be called the Hamlet of Harrisburg.

So Senator Goldwater walked away with the nomination. Mr Nixon once said that if Mr Goldwater ever had a chance to win the election, he lost it on the night of his acceptance speech.[10] With millions of people watching, he chose not to bind up the wounds of his party but to cut them deeper. 'Those who do not care for our cause we don't expect to enter our ranks in any case... Moderation in the pursuit of justice is no virtue.'[11]

The phoenix that arose out of the ashes of Goldwaterism was the career of Ronald Reagan; and its means was television. In 1954 Ronald Reagan, with a long Hollywood career as actor and union leader behind him, joined a television drama series called *The General Electric Theater* as host and occasional performer. At the same time he became a roving ambassador from the General Electric management to their quarter of a million employees. For eight years he made them all much the same speech, about the dangers of big government. Then in the autumn of 1964 he delivered a version of the speech on national television as an appeal for funds for the Goldwater campaign. The financial harvest was good: the personal harvest was better. In the words of two experienced observers, 'It was the most successful national political debut since William Jennings Bryan electrified the 1896 Democratic convention with his "Cross of Gold" speech (which also had been carefully pretested

on the lecture circuit) and it made Reagan a political star over-
night.'[12]

The day after Senator Goldwater was defeated at the polls, the
first group was formed to promote Ronald Reagan for president.
Two years later he was elected Governor of California by a majority
of nearly a million votes. When he did not always perform as
governor what he had promised as candidate, he kept his fans faithful with filmed statements for television which most local stations
were happy to use. 'On television,' said one California congressman
from the other wing of the Republican party, 'Ronald Reagan is
a demigod.'

Yet this long parade of politicians apparently pushed up or down
by television is not as conclusive as it may look. Joseph McCarthy
only began to slip in the opinion polls after the Senate had moved
against him.[18] John F. Kennedy had been an active presidential contender for nine months before the first debate with Richard Nixon.
The reaction to Richard Nixon's Checkers speech was in good measure a vote of confidence in General Eisenhower. Estes Kefauver
worked so hard at traditional campaign activity that it shortened his
life. A man as literate as Adlai Stevenson depended for his growing
fame to a great extent on written reporting. He also had President
Truman's help at the start. Robert Kennedy had his elder brother's
help. Henry Cabot Lodge had the prestige of a man who had been
successively senator, UN ambassador and vice-presidential candidate
before he went to Saigon. William Scranton, starting when he did,
had virtually no chance of winning the Republican nomination anyway. Barry Goldwater had incurred public suspicion long before he
was nominated. Ronald Reagan had made some fifty films and
countless television appearances before his Goldwater speech.

In other words, in all these instances there were other persuasions
or influences at work besides television.

Further, in a more recent and remarkable instance, damage in-
flicted on a political reputation chiefly by television was undone in
a matter of days. 'The biggest name on the casualty list from the
great "Battle of Michigan Avenue" Thursday', began a report on
the front page of the *Chicago Daily News* at the end of the 1968
Democratic convention, 'was Richard J. Daley. The mayor didn't
get his head busted by the club-swinging cops outside the Hilton
Hotel. But their performance did . . . smash Daley's exalted political
reputation into small pieces.'[14] At the time it was an entirely reason-

able view. Yet a fortnight later, even before the television showing of a film made for the Mayor which offered his brand of evidence that his police were provoked, the Federal Communications Commission asked the networks to reply to the 'hundreds of complaints' which the Commission had received about the unfairness of network television reports from Chicago. Opinion polls showed the same thing. Great numbers of viewers found it possible to exonerate Mr Daley simply by disbelieving what they had seen.

Nevertheless, however limited television's real effect on individual political fortunes, the fact that politicians believe there is an effect creates one: they choose candidates in the light of it. Once posit a belief that television is decisive, and candidates are chosen to be persuasive on television.

Members of Congress have been heard to maintain that this has made them, in the mass, a much more presentable lot than they were before the fierce light of television beat upon them. These things are hard to measure. But it is true that the 1964 and 1966 intakes into both houses of Congress did look a little like heats in a holiday-camp handsomest-man contest; and it was hard not to believe that, unless there was a biological relation between legislative ability and good looks, some of them were there chiefly because they were good-looking. Before Mrs Shirley Temple Black's defeat for the House of Representatives in November 1967 gave them pause, California Republicans had sent a retired musical-comedy performer to the Senate and an Olympic decathlon champion to the House: neither of them had even Governor Reagan's political credentials. Ohio tried an astronaut, and Oklahoma the state university's football coach. It was nothing but a good thing that other professions besides the law should be represented in American elective politics; but the other professions seemed sometimes to be chosen more for their familiarity to the television audience than their usefulness as a training.

The other reason why American politicians make more use of television than British politicians do is that the law allows them to; and the effect of this too is chiefly seen in the appointment of candidates.

In Britain, politicians cannot buy broadcast time. It is rationed. Besides what they can win on news bulletins and discussion programmes, the amount of advertising time open to them – time over which they have total editorial control – is set by an agreement between the main parties, with the concurrence of the broadcasting authorities. On the BBC's two networks and on the commercial network, in terms re-approved by Parliament in 1963 and 1964, the allocation was free; and the wealth of the Indies could not extend it, however tempted broadcasters might be to expand their operating revenues so simply.[15]

In America, despite repeated efforts, there was still no such legislation by the time the 1968 elections came round. The United States remained the only country in the world where candidates with access to the air had to pay for their use of it. There was no distribution of free political advertising time.

To make up for this, there was no prohibition of paid political advertising. The only limitations were general ones on campaign expenditure, generally disregarded. Effectively, politicians could have as much television exposure as they could pay for.

This had the theoretical consequence that any voice could be heard which had the money to back it; and to that extent freedom of speech was protected. It also had a more rapid practical consequence. Since useful television time was not cheap, some candidates spent large sums. Since no self-denying ordinance will work where the law does not, all candidates for important jobs then had to spend large sums. But there was no established source of these sums except the candidate himself.

There had been wealthy politicians and wealthy presidents before television. Television simply gave wealth a new importance. Received opinion about the effects of television made it very desirable that a candidate should be handsome: the state of broadcasting law made it very desirable that he should be rich.

John F. Kennedy, the ideal candidate of the sixties, was the apotheosis of these attributes; and he used them both to advantage. In the crucial West Virginia primary of May 1960 Hubert Humphrey almost bankrupted himself in spending less than a tenth of what was laid out on the Kennedy victory.

Although President Johnson had not needed television to come to power in the first place, he was by then a very wealthy man; and although he had fewer natural gifts for television than the man he succeeded, he none the less laboured mightily at acquiring them. He was never good-looking: one American writer not trammelled by working in Washington called him 'as homely as you can get without being asked not to loiter'.[16] The qualities that made him a potent force in person, the large gestures and earthy speech, were necessarily unsuitable on television. There is his wife's authority for this view. 'I do think that he is at his best in a small group of people where he simply talks straight from the heart. There's a pungency and a colour and a humour and a force in meetings of that sort, and it may be equally as good in a face-to-face confrontation with a larger group. It is somewhat diluted and restricted when it gets to the mechanics of TV and the great invisible audience.'[17]

Yet the president totally overcame these restrictions in the March 1968 broadcasts where he came to the end of what he had to say about his efforts for peace in Vietnam and continued: 'I do not believe that I should devote an hour or a day of my time to any personal partisan causes ... Accordingly I shall not seek, and I will not accept, the nomination of my party for another term as your president.' A man who had not always been believed found a way to be believed and respected then.

President Johnson's first attempt at television talk – in imitation of the fireside-chat vein of his first mentor, President Franklin Roosevelt – had been in March 1964, four months after President Kennedy's death brought him to power; and it was not considered a success. He fell back on the standard televised press conference; but there was continuous experiment with lights, mobile microphones, teleprompters, spectacles (including contact lenses) and make-up. For his 1968 state-of-the-union message he appeared in the House chamber with his hair perceptibly wavy. His press secretary said afterwards that the wave was natural.

Favourable comment on a televised White House press conference in November 1967 encouraged him to try the fireside formula again, with three interrogators and his wife beside him, on the limited subject of his daughter Lynda's impending wedding; and this in turn emboldened him to take the same three network reporters on over an hour's course and a wider range of questions. Over fifty million people saw the broadcast. Unfortunately the scene they remembered best was one where the President insisted on interviewing the ABC man, Frank Reynolds, about the problem of the cities. ('What is your answer to it, Frank?' 'Well, I would hope that – I don't know that my answer is necessarily the one, sir, that we want.' 'What is your answer, though, Frank?' – and the question was put twice more. The incident conferred a kind of fame, and the president took credit for Mr Reynolds's subsequent promotion at ABC.)

None of the serious contenders for the President's job in 1968 could get so much useful exposure without paying for it. The money did not necessarily come out of their own pockets; but campaign life was damagingly inconvenient for candidates with no easy command of wealth – their own or other people's. Shortage of money during the primaries more than once made Senator McCarthy forfeit television time and leave the field altogether while he went to New York in search of subscriptions.

It was the Republican party which had the most remarkable array of candidates with the television talents. From the November 1966 elections onward, five men were commonly mentioned. Four of them, besides acceptable looks and voices, had considerable personal wealth: Governor Romney of Michigan and Senator Percy of Illinois as a result of success in midwestern business, Governor Rockefeller of New York hereditarily and on a larger scale, Governor Reagan of California through film earnings well invested in land. Only Mr Nixon was not a handsome millionaire. But even he had been earning $200,000 a year as a Wall Street lawyer, and on television he had at any rate what the professionals called 'identification': the moment he came on the screen you knew who it was.

All these men were elected or re-elected to their jobs in November 1966. The rules on disclosing campaign expenditures are undemanding, and the FCC's published figures unrevealing. In those elections, though, at least a third of a million dollars appears to have been spent on television advertising for Senator Percy, a million for Governor Reagan and a million and a quarter for Governor Rockefeller. Candidates for the Senate in 1968 were told by their advertising agencies that television time would cost them ten cents for every man, woman and child in the state. This meant that senatorial candidates in six states could expect to pay at least a million dollars or run the risk of losing. In California and New York the sum would be nearer two million. And this allowed nothing for the cost of producing the advertisements, which commonly added a quarter to the cost of buying the time for them.

There may have been senatorial candidates who could contemplate these sums. An Associated Press survey in March 1968 suggested that between twenty and thirty of the hundred senators then serving were millionaires. Wealthy or not, politicians still bore peculiar burdens in paying these enormous sums. Although the law said that they were not to be charged more than other advertisers,[18] it happened: no campaign lasted long enough for a candidate to qualify for the complicated series of discounts which broadcasters gave their regular customers. Further, politicians were one of the few classes of advertiser from whom broadcasting and advertising organisations demanded payment in advance, because political bad debts could not be set against tax. Senator Vance Hartke once got his money to an Indiana broadcasting station only just in time to stop them cancelling his broadcast.

Candidates in presidential as distinct from state elections had all these problems multiplied by at least fifty. Senator Goldwater's campaign for the presidency in 1964, when he was defeated by the biggest margin ever recorded, was the most expensive ever recorded: it cost over $19 million. About a third of that went on television.

The total sums made over to political advertising space on television have been remarkable, even without reckoning anything for production costs. In 1952 the declared figure for all candidates, presidential as well, was $3 million, not counting primaries. In 1956 the comparable figure was $6.6 million: in 1960, $10 million; and in 1964, $17.5 million.[19] Including primaries, air time for television politics in 1964 cost nearly $24 million.[20] The FCC put the proportion spent directly on the presidential campaign in that year at 42 per cent, or nearly $10 million; with the other $14 million spent on behalf of other candidates.

By 1966, when there was no presidential campaign, this last figure had risen to nearly $19 million.[21] To this must be added over $13 million for radio advertising; giving a grand total for broadcast advertising, without production costs, of more than $32 million. It already seemed probable that in 1968 this figure would reach $50 million, with over $20 million of it spent in pursuit of the presidency. The Nixon broadcast campaign alone was to cost at least $8 million.

These sums did not entirely represent an increase in the use of broadcast advertising: there had also been an increase in its expense. Rates went up by an average of 30 or 40 per cent between 1961 and 1967. But those were the sums which political advertisers paid. They represented an incubus on political activity not paralleled anywhere else in the world.

This aspect of the effect of television on politics in America was summed up in senate testimony by the man Charles Percy beat, Paul Douglas, who had been an Illinois senator for eighteen years. 'It is clear that it is almost impossible for a poor man to run for public office, and that a man of moderate means can only do so if he has the backing of men and forces of great wealth.'[22]

Mr Douglas wanted it clear that he had no prejudice against the rich as such. He quoted the lines from *Iolanthe*: 'Hearts just as pure and fair May beat in Belgrave Square As in the lowly air Of Seven Dials'. The fact remained that people who were not rich had to think long and hard before they made an attempt on public office of any importance. One man who had been narrowly defeated for the lieutenant-governorship of Texas settled down after the election to pay off campaign debts out of a civil service salary at a rate which would take him nineteen years.

So there is a danger that the cost of campaigning, chiefly swollen by the cost of television, will exclude the honest poor. A more serious danger for American politics is that it does not always exclude the dishonest poor.

If a candidate cannot meet his election expenses himself, he has to get other people to help him. The federal government does not help him, although there have been repeated suggestions that it should. His party, at a national level, does not help him a great deal: private contributors, giving their own money, very seldom contribute enough. The chief source left is business. Properly conducted business houses do not as a rule spend money without expecting some advantage in return. Politicians in a hurry or in difficulties may sometimes have to see that they get it.

Companies are forbidden by law from contributing to campaign funds.[23] But many companies pay high salaries at the top, and allow their senior people to run heavy expense accounts. The company chairman decides that a certain candidate must be helped to win; often because he is an important member of the congressional committee that regulates the affairs of the industry which the company is part of. The candidate gives a dinner to raise funds, at $100 a plate. In case any of the company's senior staff are thinking of staying away, the chairman invites them to stop at his house or his hotel room for a drink on the way to the dinner. They take the point. They have to regard it as one of the things that they are paid a high salary for.

Corporations can contribute more directly to party funds by taking advertising space at ten or fifteen thousand dollars a page in party brochures. Defence contractors do it: so do airlines and railway companies. Organisations that do business with the government, or need its permission to do other business of their own, can always use a friendly voice in Congress.

Senator Russell Long of Louisiana, from a family and a state that understands political persuasion, spelled out the *quid pro quo* at the local level from the chair of the Senate Finance Committee in June 1967. 'I have seen men start out running for governor with the firm intention of promising nothing. Coming down the stretch, I have seen them making commitments that it made me sick to see. They did it because they could not pay for radio and television. Their sign boards were taken down, and the only way they could cross that finish line and make a respectable showing was to make promises they did not want to make, such as promising the highway contractors who the contract would be given to; promising the insurance companies as to who the insurance commissioner would be.'[24]

The cost of television has materially increased the dangers of corruption in American public life. But they were there before. They have long enjoyed a certain tolerance as the fellow-travellers of free enterprise. After a Treasury official had told Senator Long's committee that 'the threat to political morality is becoming greater every day', Senator Eugene McCarthy suddenly interjected: 'A Kansas poet has written that "if we purify the pond, the lilies die".'[25]

Television does not therefore seem to have had quite the effect on American political life and fortunes it is commonly credited with. The case for television as a determining element in political success is not made. On the other hand, the belief that television wields determining powers has had a bearing on the kind of candidate who is given the opportunity to stand for election; and so has the cost of television. In addition, the cost has sometimes affected the behaviour of politicians once elected.

PART IV

Television and Governments

10 Electoral Television and the Law

The problems of election broadcasting in America and Britain are not lessened by the state of the law.

In America, most candidates for senior office have for some time been spending more on television alone than the law intends them to spend on their whole campaign. This is not as serious a consequence of election television as the fact that it chooses candidates on narrow grounds, or that it bankrupts some, or that it corrupts some. The chief conclusion that follows from it is that the law needs changing. Yet a state of affairs where out-of-date laws are neither honoured nor altered by the men who make laws is no encouragement to the rule of law.

The federal law on election spending dates from an epoch when both broadcasting and advertising were still undeveloped areas. Under a statute passed in 1925 and not much amended since, a candidate for senator could spend a maximum of $25,000 in the campaign, and for congressman $5000;[1] or less, if the state law set a lower limit. In Ohio in 1968 even a candidate for the Senate was held to $5000.

After the election, the secretary of the Senate or the clerk of the House was to be told what had been spent. But a candidate only had to report spending which had his knowledge and consent: committees raising funds on his behalf were only asked to make a report at all if they existed in more than one state, which few committees concerned with an election to Congress found necessary. The law also said nothing about spending in primary elections.

The upshot was that the law was cheerfully flouted. During his 1967 enquiries into campaign financing, Senator Russell Long of Louisiana asked the Comptroller General of the United States whether he knew offhand what the spending limits were for a Louisiana senate race. The Comptroller General said he did not. 'I can't tell you,' the Senator said, 'and I couldn't care less. I understand how you get around that act, and so does everybody else who has been elected three or four times.'[2]

Presidential campaign spending was in theory brought under control fifteen years later by an amended act which applied to any candidate for an elective federal office. Nobody could contribute more than $5000 in a year to any one candidate or committee, and no one committee could spend more than $3 million a year.[3] But certain kinds of primary were not covered: local committees were again not covered; and there was no limit on the number of committees that might exist.

It is the managers for Wendell Willkie, as Republican candidate for president in 1940, who are credited with having first seen the significance of this last point – when the ink was scarcely dry on the new provisions. They began what became the unvarying practice of having a multiplicity of committees. 'Artists and entertainers for Johnson-Humphrey' or 'Pharmacists for Johnson-Humphrey' did not band together solely to offer independent witness: they were also encouraged to do it because it was a way of breaking down support for the Democratic candidates into groups whose separate contributions would all fall just below the legal limit.

President Johnson was as aware of the absurdity as anyone. Both in 1966 and 1967 he commended to Congress election reform acts which would have done away with spending limits and enforced proper disclosure. Neither became law.

No candidate had ever been prosecuted for flouting the rules on federal elections; and for local offices the position was at least as anarchic. No candidate for the governorship of New York was supposed to spend more than $20,000.[4] It was the virtual impossibility of showing that a candidate had 'knowingly aided or participated' in the spending of money on his behalf which allowed Nelson Rockefeller's managers in 1966 to make no secret of expenses which went over $5 million.

Other things besides television have raised the cost of electioneering. Easier travel has not meant cheaper travel. Computers for mailing lists are expensive. Political poll-takers have become the chartered accountants of the electoral business, and charge as much for their services. Yet these developments have been known in Britain too; and there the problems of paying for election campaigns have been nothing like so acute. The spending limits written into the

Representation of the People Act of 1949 were in fact lower, even in money terms, than they had been in 1918.[5] On a system which took account of the population and type of each constituency, the most favoured parliamentary candidates in the 1966 election could spend scarcely more than £1300.

In the post-election reports made by candidates' agents there is some misrepresentation: the comparative shortness of a British election campaign, in particular, makes it easy to pay for election services before or after the period of their use. But the scale of this deceit is small. And the chief difference is that there can be no spending on television.

Yet Britain has not escaped this problem of the cost of political television at election times under existing law. It arose in another form, where it gave more trouble to broadcasters than politicians.

Section 63 of the 1949 Representation of the People Act forbade 'any person other than the candidate, his election agent and persons authorised in writing by the election agent' to spend money in presenting a candidate or his views or the extent of his backing to the electors. But mention of the candidate in newspapers or on the air presented him to the electors, and cost money: more money, properly reckoned, than a candidate might spend in all. Parliament provided that the prohibition should not 'restrict the publication of any matter relating to the election in a newspaper or other periodical'; but by a remarkable oversight, although at the time the act was passed the BBC had been broadcasting television programmes uninterruptedly for three years and radio programmes for twenty-seven, nothing at all was said about broadcasting. On a strict reading of the act almost any broadcast election reporting, however unevaluative, could convict 'a director, general manager, secretary or other similar officer' of the broadcasting organisation of a corrupt practice; which could afflict him with a number of disabilities, among them as much as a year in prison.[6]

Since broadcasting chiefs were no readier than anyone else would be to value the people's right to know above their own liberty, the broadcast reporting of elections was marked for several years by extreme caution. But elections were there, and they had to be covered, however unclear the law. The impulse to bolder and more rapid experiment came from the rivalry engendered when commercial television began in 1955. In 1958 Granada Television, the ITV company whose franchise then covered most of the north of England, put all three candidates on the air in a by-election at Rochdale. No one complained. In the general election the following year the BBC, with their hearts in their mouths, allowed their news broadcasters to quote campaign speeches for the first time; and they mounted sound and television programmes in which representative politicians argued with representative voters. Except for two brief snatches, they never showed sound film of candidates campaigning in their own constituencies; and it was late in the campaign before ITN got permission from the Independent Television Authority to report on a specific constituency by that method.

Granada extended their earlier innovation. In a series of programmes called *Election Marathon*, they marshalled the candidates for a hundred seats in their area into brief studio debates, seat by seat. Not all constituencies were covered, because not all candidates were willing or able. Granada had taken legal opinion from the Master of Trinity Hall at Cambridge, Sir Ivor Jennings; and he had adjudged it a first condition of remaining within the law that 'no candidate should appear on television unless all the other candidates in his constituency are prepared to appear'.[7]

This ruling was scrupulously observed, then and for four years afterwards. Broadcasters had nothing much else to go on, and they were anxious to be fair. The difficulty was to be sure what was fair. They knew what was fair for political advertising time, because the parties told them: since 1939 a block of time had been thrown to the three main parties to divide as they thought fit, and the broadcasting authorities did not need to trouble their heads about whether the arrangement bore hardly on minor parties or the audience. But away from these blessed certainties fairness was a much more elusive quality.

The discovery that nothing is fair to everyone in politics was made in two successive elections by opponents of Sir Alec Douglas-Home. In the by-election that brought Sir Alec back to the House of Commons in November 1963, at Kinross and West Perthshire, the only one of the main candidates who lived in the division was the Liberal, Alastair Duncan Millar. He was a landowner and hence an employer of labour. The territory was the most safely Conservative as well as the handsomest in Scotland; but the Liberals were making ground in Scotland at the time, and voters in those parts were believed to prefer a candidate whom they were accustomed to respect, and Mr Duncan

Millar believed that he might win the seat if he could keep his advantage as the candidate best known locally. This advantage was threatened by television. The newspaper coverage was bad enough, with a cavalcade of journalists following Sir Alec everywhere he went along the narrow Perthshire roads and relegating his opponents to the small print at the foot of their copy; but the last straw was a proposal by ITN to film interviews of equal length, in what had become a standard by-election practice, with all the candidates – including the miscellaneous independent candidates attracted into a contest where one candidate was a prime minister. Although we pursued him down the cobbled streets of Crieff, Mr Duncan Millar refused us an interview, in the belief that under the Jennings rule the item could not then go forward. ITN nevertheless decided in London that it should. Where the other candidates were shown talking on film, he was represented by still pictures and a reading from his manifesto. It must have made very little difference: television reception on the commercial channel was in any case poor in Perthshire at that time; but Mr Duncan Millar did not win the by-election, and did not present a petition against the result, and the perimeter within which television could legally operate at elections had been pushed a little further outward.

When he defended his seat in the general election less than a year later, Sir Alec had no Liberal opponent, but he had a Communist instead. The Communists had long felt that the system of party political broadcasts was unfair to them; and their candidate, Dr C. M. Grieve, meant to test it in the courts. Under the name of Hugh McDiarmid he was a Scottish poet of some repute, and he made fun of Sir Alec's title to be thought either a Scotsman or a farmer – 'couldn't cultivate a window-box', he said of him in a speech in Hyde Park before the campaign. As a candidate he did no more than he needed: when I interviewed him a few days before polling I found him fifty miles outside the constituency at his cottage in the Lanarkshire hills.

After his defeat he petitioned against Sir Alec's election. He leant his case on the Conservative party political broadcasts during the campaign. Sir Alec, as party leader, had appeared in the first of them for two minutes and in the fifth for fifteen. They were networked nationally by both the BBC and ITV. Dr Grieve's contention was that the Corporation and the Independent Television Authority had broken the law because they had spent money presenting Sir Alec and his views to the electors of Kinross and West Perthshire without the written authority of his agent.

The Communist point, which won a good deal of sympathy, was that the fortunes of Sir Alec as Conservative leader could not realistically be separated from his fortunes as an individual Conservative candidate. An Election Court in Edinburgh found that they could: Sir Alec's election was upheld, and the Communists' only achievement had been to clear yet another area of legal imprecision. The judges agreed that Sir Alec might have derived local advantage from these broadcasts; but they also agreed with the broadcasters' submission that the broadcasts had only been mounted to inform the electorate at large.

It follows that if free political advertising time is in the best interests of the electorate, then the interests of the electorate and of some candidates are unavoidably in conflict.

The problem has never arisen in this form in America, since there is no authorised and prearranged allowance of free party time. If there is any at all, it is only by the generosity of individual networks and stations. Further, the situation is different in America in at least two ways.

One is that a party leader, in the sense of a presidential candidate, is not at the same time appealing for the votes of a particular territorial subdivision of the nation. His name, or a list of the names of electors expected to vote for him, is on the ballot in every district of every state in the union; whereas in Britain a party leader's name is only on the ballot-paper in a single constituency, the one he seeks to represent in the Commons. There is therefore not the same problem in America of a local candidate getting an uncovenanted advantage because he is also a national candidate.

(It has happened. When Senator Lyndon Johnson campaigned for the vice-presidency in 1960, he was also defending his Texas senate seat, just in case. He held it, and then resigned it in January 1961. But the state law had been changed to make this double candidacy possible. In 1964 Senator Goldwater had secured no such fallback position in Arizona, and spent the next four years as a private citizen.)

The other point of difference in America is that local and national candidates are not necessarily fighting the same election. In every presidential election year there are several candidates for governor or senator or congressman who are at pains to mark their separation from a locally unpopular presidential candidate of the same party. Several Democratic candidates for the Senate in the autumn of 1968 put as much ground as they could between themselves and Mr Humphrey. So if there were nationally ordained party broadcasts, they would have to relate much more to how people voted for president and vice president than for local offices.

There has been repeated pressure for some system of free time for candidates on television, mainly because of the side consequences of its being at present so expensive. The chiefs of the broadcasting industry are not in favour. They say they would be happy to contribute free time if they were not in danger of having to waste it on a throng of frivolous candidates. The available evidence is not kind to this account of their own motives. The interest which the industry took in the 1960 presidential debates was not renewed for debates at any lower level. According to a 1962 survey, candidates in straight fights for the Senate got free time from rather fewer of the television stations analysed than candidates who had minor-party opposition as well: 23 per cent as against 26 per cent.[8]

The reason why candidates have small hope of any free time laid down by law lies in the powerlessness of the Federal Communications Commission. It is, in its own words, 'the United States Government agency charged with regulating interstate and foreign communication by means of radio, wire and cable'; and it is the most denounced of all federal regulatory agencies – outside the broadcasting industry for not raising its voice more loudly, and inside the industry for raising it at all. The Commission's nominal sanction against broadcasting stations which neglect politics or commit any other sin is not to renew their licences. The sanction has been very seldom invoked on any grounds. In practice the Commission's only instrument in the matter of broadcast time for political candidates is section 315a of the Communications Act. The section obliges a broadcaster who puts one candidate on the air to 'afford equal opportunities to all other such candidates for that office', unless the first appearance was in a specified kind of news programme. This means in effect that if he sells time to one candidate, he has to allow the others to buy the same amount if they want it; or to have it for nothing, if the first man had it for nothing. But he need not let any of them have any time at all, paid or free, as long as his refusals are impartial.

This piece of law, first passed in 1934 and tinkered with in 1959, has been the base for as much metaphysical argument as the passage in British law about election expenses. Even before it was waived by law for the period of the 1960 campaign to make the Nixon-Kennedy debates two-sided instead of sixteen-sided, it had been endlessly glossed by the FCC in a series of letters and telegrams to broadcasting stations and aggrieved candidates.[9]

A television station in Scranton, Pennsylvania, employed a man who – without being seen on the screen – read the words of station announcements and advertisements. In 1965 he wanted to become a candidate for a local borough council. If he did, would his opponents be entitled to a share in the work? The FCC thought not. But he was also the host of a weekly dance party; and if he did that during the campaign, the other candidates would then have a right to an equal length of free time. The opponents of a 'weathercaster' in Waco, on the other hand, who was defending his seat in the lower house of the Texas legislature, had no redress against his extra exposure. That 1960 ruling was upheld in the courts.

Much of this logic-chopping has related to presidential campaigns. The Commission ruled in the autumn of 1964 that televised press conferences or even charitable appeals by President Johnson would entitle his opponent, Senator Goldwater, to equal time; but that the President's televised report to the nation about the Chinese nuclear bomb and the fall of Mr Khrushchev less than three weeks before polling did not. This last decision was narrowly upheld in the courts. Yet the Senator never stood in more need of equal broadcasting opportunity. If he was to stay a plausible candidate he had to refute exactly the charge which these events gave weight to: that the world was too dangerous a place to let him loose in.

At the time the Republicans made use of the FCC's refusal as a ground for appealing for funds with which to answer the President; but afterwards Mr Goldwater often complained of the disadvantage.

The argument was renewed, with similar results, in the run-up to the 1968 elections. In December 1967 the three networks gave the congressional leadership of the Republican party opportunity to reply to attacks on them which the President had made in a speech to a trade union audience in Florida. The networks had been induced to cover the speech live without knowing what was in it. A month later they arranged for various forms of Republican reply to the President's state-of-the-union message before it had even been delivered. Neither opportunity was well taken, and on the chief divisive issue of the time – Vietnam – the Republicans supported the President anyway. He will have had no cause to quarrel with the networks' decision.

But the broadcasting authorities took a different line when they were challenged in the early days of his campaign by Senator Eugene McCarthy; and the decision will have been even more satisfactory to the President, since the Senator's main aim at that time was to give opposition to the Vietnam war some chance of expression at the polls. Four days after the networks had allowed the Republicans their reply to the Florida speech, President Johnson implied in his White House interview with three network reporters that Senator McCarthy was in league with Senator Robert Kennedy and that both men were chiefly driven by ambition. At that time the prospect that the President would not himself stand again was taken seriously by no one: not even, on the evidence of his actions, by the President himself.

Senator McCarthy's campaign manager, Blair Clark, sent telegrams to the three networks claiming the right of reply. He reminded them that the law prescribed equal opportunities for all candidates for the same public office: President Johnson's public statements left little doubt that he would be a candidate for president in 1968, and the newspaper advertising of the broadcast 'made it a most obvious campaign effort'.

CBS, for whom Mr Clark used to work, turned the request down: the President was not a legally qualified candidate, and he had made no attack on the Senator. The other two networks followed. On the Senator's behalf Mr Clark complained to the FCC: every American child knew that the President was a candidate. The FCC thereupon allowed their reading of where the power lay to be a little too apparent. For answer they sent Mr Clark, without a covering letter, two pamphlets on FCC policy.

Senator McCarthy sent the Chairman of the Commission a telegram to say that 'this casual and offhand way of handling public business is an outrage'. The Chairman replied that the pamphlets had been put in the post before Mr Clark's complaint had arrived: a staff member had been trying to be helpful. The Senator's lawyers claimed in a formal petition to the FCC that the President was indeed a candidate, because he and his staff were already working on four primaries. After another fortnight's deliberation the FCC maintained their view that the law only applied to announced candidates. The Senator's lawyer said it was a sad day when an independent federal agency 'knuckles down to presidential power'. The courts agreed with the FCC.

The fact is that election-time television is very difficult territory for lawyers and commissioners and judges. Equity is often unattainable.

The Public Broadcast Laboratory first went on the air from New York in November 1967 with three hours of television on the problems of race. The first broadcast fell just before run-off elections for mayor in one or two important American cities, notably Cleveland and Boston. PBL covered the straight fight in Boston with scarcely a look at the personable Irishman who went on to win, Kevin White. They devoted nearly all their time to his opponent, Mrs Louise Day Hicks: a large, thin-lipped woman whose slogan, 'You know where I stand', was widely understood in Boston as a promise not to indulge the city's Negroes. PBL wanted to show people what she was like. The programme was seen in Boston. Was it equally fair to both candidates? Neither complained, nor did more than a few viewers. People who feared Mrs Hicks and people who looked to her in hope were for the most part pleased at this extra insight into her views.

So there are times when a manifest imbalance seems fair. Equally there are times when a scrupulous balance seems unfair. During British general elections, television news people spend a great deal of effort on making sure that the total time devoted to spokesmen of the two main parties is the same. One Conservative who filled a large share of his party's time in the 1964 election was Quintin Hogg. There could be no grounds for complaint in that: he had recently been a favoured candidate for the party leadership, and he was still a cabinet minister. But much of what was reported of Mr Hogg was the aftermath of his suggestion that there were adulterers on the Labour front bench, which embarrassed his own party more than Labour. Television journalists asked one another in some perplexity: 'Whose time does Hogg come out of?'

Most American broadcasters have one freedom which British broadcasters do not: they are allowed to back specific candidates in much the same way that newspapers do. There is nothing to prevent their saying in station editorials, though not in their news coverage, which candidate has their support.

When the BBC were given their first licence for ten years from the beginning of 1927, the postmaster-general of the day gave them two general prohibitions: that they should not broadcast their own opinion on matters of public policy, and that they should not broadcast on matters of political, industrial or religious controversy. The second prohibition was withdrawn the next year. The first has been maintained: it is a continuing condition of the licence to broadcast, renewed with the licence by letter from the postmaster-general in office at the time. The same condition was written into the act that established commercial television in Britain in 1954, and kept in later versions.[10]

In America the only broadcasters under the same limitation are the ones operating non-commercial stations with the help of federal money from the Corporation for Public Broadcasting, which was established in November 1967.[11] Other stations may say what they like as long as they identify it as their own opinion. What is interesting is the sparing use made of this freedom. During the 1964 elections, only 17 of the 661 television stations then on the air reported broadcasting editorials for or against any candidates. In 1966 the proportion was 21 out of 721.[12] The reason was not so much that stations preferred their political space paid for as that they preferred to avoid the wearisome disputes with local politicians and the FCC which editorialising might get them into.

It is not only the voice of the broadcaster that is stilled in both countries at election times. The chief voice unheard is the voice of the voter.

A traditional technique of television reporting is to stop people in the street and ask them what they think about some issue of the day. It is awkward work for the questioner, but – except at the extremes of the social scale – more people than not are prepared to try and answer difficult questions from a total stranger if he has a microphone in his hand; and if there is a little variety in the questioning, and if all but a sentence or two of each answer is thrown away in the cutting, the results can have considerable value as entertainment and even some small value as evidence.

(These interviews are sometimes called vox pops, as an abbreviation for *vox populi vox Dei*. The phrase came from the BBC, and could have originated nowhere else. No other organisation is so keenly aware that the last place to listen for the voice of God is in the voice of the people: no other organisation could pass off the sad necessity of none the less bending an ear in that direction with a Latin joke.)

But the voice of the people is little better than a nuisance under current broadcasting law. Stopping a man in the street is not what in America the Communications Act calls a bona-fide news event, and gives no release from the obligation 'to afford reasonable opportunity for the discussion of conflicting views on issues of public importance'. But the man in the street might not understand this: he might be in danger of saying what he thought, to the detriment of what in Britain the Representation of the People Act calls due impartiality. In ordinary circumstances the balance can be restored later, if need be; but during a campaign the time is short and the protest from the side who think themselves under-represented is instant. Far better to confine the humble voter to his proper function: humbly voting.

At the outset of the 1964 general election campaign in Britain, I interviewed several West Indians, Indians and Pakistanis who had come to live in the Sparkbrook division of Birmingham, which was at that time in Conservative hands. Virtually all those whose answers could be understood declared that they would vote Labour. This was not without interest for the future, at a time when public discussion was concentrating on how other voters would react to immigrants rather than on how immigrants themselves would vote; and it was statistically not unsound, in that four weeks later Labour took Sparkbrook with the highest straight movement of opinion in the West Midlands. But it was unfit for public showing. The voters of Sparkbrook had not shown due impartiality.

The case is not covered by British law about the secrecy of the ballot, which applies only to what happens to actual ballot papers, either at polling stations or in the hands of postal voters or proxies. But this section of the law is allowed to inhibit television in another way.

In a British election, the climactic drama in each constituency is the counting of the votes. This is not true to the same extent in America, where a good many votes – though not yet a majority – are cast and therefore counted by machine; and whether they are or not, results are let out piecemeal, there is no formal declaration of the polls, and the most charged moment is the defeated candidate's concession, which may be a long time coming. But in Britain a good count is as good as a play.

Under the creaking rafters of some corn exchange or moot hall, no sound is heard except the susurration of unnumbered ballot-papers in the process of being numbered by scores of hands (mostly belonging to bank tellers making a little money on the side). On the bare trestle tables the ballots cast for each candidate gradually multiply in small square piles of a hundred votes each. The candidates themselves stalk up and down between the tables, their faces livid with fatigue and tension above their rosettes. Messengers stumble in from outlying areas with fresh votes in black tin boxes. At the centre of the scene the clerk to the local council, as acting returning officer, collates the totals and confers in whispers with his staff. At last he summons the candidates; but it is only to ask for their agreement to his ruling on disputed ballot-papers. They are in a state to agree to anything. Finally he arrays them round him and clears his throat. 'The number of votes cast...'

Even the unity of time has been neatly preserved: with seldom more than sixty thousand votes to count, a clerk who cares about these things can get done in an hour. The same for the unity of place: all the action has unrolled within the view of a single television camera.

But often, even in the most vital contests, there has not been a camera there; or if there has, it has not been allowed to show even the most general shot of the piles of ballot-papers. Similarly the reporter who is there to talk about what the camera sees is told that he may not say 'The Conservative piles are now a little more numerous than the Labour piles.' Yet all the law forbids is that anyone attending the count should find out the number on the back of a paper, or should 'communicate any information...as to the candidate for whom any vote is given on any particular ballot paper'.[13] The source of the more detailed restrictions on television, which sometimes extend to excluding the cameras altogether, is simply three typed, duplicated and undated pages of 'notes for the guidance of returning officers' put out by the Home Office; and the authority which council clerks rely on to enforce them is no more than their power as acting returning officers to exclude whom they will from the count.[14] The progress of election counts, legitimately a matter of intense public interest, has been made known in the United States without ill effect for years.

The last topic to which elected representatives are ready to address themselves is any reform of the system which saw them safely elected. When the Speaker's Conference on Electoral Law reported to the Prime Minister in February 1968, its members specifically decided to make no recommendation on the question of 'whether the law should be amended so as to limit the returning officer's discretion to permit arrangements to be made for the broadcasting of any part of the proceedings at the count'.[15] The report betrayed no knowledge of the fact that the law did not give him this discretion. The new Representation of the People Bill approved by the Commons in December 1968 simply stiffened the arm of the returning officer as chucker-out: he could exclude anyone he thought might impede efficient vote-counting. Nothing was said about what television people would be allowed to report if they got inside. The new bill gave parliamentary candidates another £300 to spend, and it added television and radio to newspapers and periodicals as places where a candidate's views could be presented without his being held accountable for the expense. But the bill resanctified the Jennings rule: a candidate could once again veto joint constituency broadcasts by refusing to take part in them or to let them go ahead without him. Although it was the first piece of British election law which took any account of the existence of television, it was in the end no more helpful than the body of FCC philosophisings to which American broadcasters looked.

11 Velvet Glove

The interest of television in politicians does not end with elections, nor of politicians in television. So the rules reach wider than elections. It is at election times that the rules governing television coverage of politics are most frequently appealed to and most eagerly applied; but they are still current in the period between elections.

All governments control broadcasters in some measure, if only to the extent of seeing that they stay off other people's frequencies. How much they control their reporting of events is a matter of philosophy and temperament.

A party of Russian government servants on a visit to the United Nations in the mid-sixties were shown film of the General Assembly incident in October 1960 when Nikita Khrushchev took his shoe off and beat his desk with it during a speech of Harold Macmillan's. It is one of the few good television pictures ever to come out of a deliberative assembly. The Russians had never seen it before.

That kind of oblivion can return to plague the inventor. One of the most important events in Mr Khrushchev's life, and indeed in modern Russian history, was his secret speech to the twentieth party congress in 1956, when he told part of the truth about Joseph Stalin. It was the beginning of Russia's slow emancipation from tyranny. In the autumn of 1967, three years after Mr Khrushchev's fall, Soviet television began showing a series of programmes to commemorate fifty years of revolution. They contrived to put together an hour's film about the year 1956 without once mentioning him.

Successive French governments have gone some distance down the same beguiling path. For the presidential election in November and December 1965 a candidates' broadcasting code was laid down by a National Control Commission guided by the Prime Minister and the Minister of Information. The ORTF gave each of General de Gaulle's five opponents two half-hours of television time and four quarter-hours. But there were close limits on what they could put into it. No film; not even still photographs; no backers from outside the candidate's own party, no supporters from unions or professional bodies, no wives; just the candidate and a few party cronies talking in a studio. It was a masterly formula for uncompelling television. And to see that it was observed, and that the candidates did not, in the official phrase, 'forget the prudence which is always necessary for those who use national communications media of such great reach', the members of the control commission could watch and edit the recorded broadcasts before they went out.

With this machinery to nullify his opponents' efforts, General de Gaulle had planned to make virtually no use of television in asking for another seven years as president. His plans were changed by the youngest of his opponents. Jean Lecanuet went into the campaign as the obscure head of a Catholic party of the centre, the Mouvement Républicain Populaire. Within ten days he was the best-known television performer on the ORTF. Laying aside his rimless glasses to disclose the crinkles round his eyes, he re-introduced the famished French to the sweets of opposition. General de Gaulle had been a hero, said Mr Lecanuet, but his policies were isolating and weakening the country, and he must give way to a younger man. The analogy with the Eisenhower-Kennedy succession five years before was much played on.

Television rental firms in Paris did better business than they had done even when the Olympic Games were relayed from Tokyo the year before. In this atmosphere, General de Gaulle's predicted share of the poll fell in a month from 66 per cent to a figure well below the 50 per cent he needed for an outright victory. Two defensive talks on television could not save him. His final score was 44 per cent. M. Mitterrand, for the united left, won 32 per cent: M. Lecanuet himself only half that. In the run-off with M. Mitterrand a fortnight later the General won by 55 per cent to 45 per cent; but only after he had given three long television interviews – a form he had never before condescended to.

General de Gaulle rightly concluded that his difficulties had arisen not so much from M. Lecanuet's *beaux yeux* as from the re-appearance of dissent on television, without much counter-argument. Even with the National Control Commission watching, the gesture had been too generous. He did not make the same mistake again. For the parliamentary elections in March 1967 there were no sentimentalities about equal time for each opposition party. Under an amendment to the electoral law pushed through the National Assembly, half the allotted broadcast time was to go to the Gaullists and half to be divided between everybody else.

Not content with that, the General used a number of devices to get an extra ration for his own side. Before the allocations took effect, he and his prime minister M. Pompidou both made political broadcasts. On the ORTF news bulletins a day's strike by eight million workers was scarcely mentioned, while a Gaullist rally was reported down to the last platitude. Ministers became extraordinarily busy at opening schools and roads and sports centres; and the ORTF felt obliged to cover them until the opposition parties protested. General de Gaulle made an eve-of-the-poll broadcast which was again outside the allocations. Europe No. 1, the commercial radio station which transmits to France from Saarbrücken in Germany, arranged a discussion of the broadcast between government and opposition figures: the government members were forbidden to take part, and the discussion had to be cancelled. With all this, the Gaullists only held on to the Assembly by the narrowest margin.

The iron hand of government was even more firmly felt after the uprising of May 1968. For a heady eleven days ORTF journalists contrived to give some account of what the protesters said and did. By the twelfth day the ORTF's government-installed management had re-asserted itself. Leaders of the broadcasting unions announced that they could no longer guarantee the objectivity of the *Journal Télévisé*, and great numbers of journalists and technicians walked off the job. But enough *jaunes* (blacklegs) could be found to operate some sort of service; and after the strike had finally collapsed in July, sixty-eight reputable journalists were dismissed and nine exiled to the provinces. It was the sign that nothing much had changed in France after all.

This degree of government control could not be more foreign to the United States. Constitutionally, the hand of government on broadcasting is kept deliberately light. The principle is as old as the First Amendment to the Constitution, contained in the 1791 Bill of Rights: 'Congress shall make no law . . . abridging the freedom of speech, or of the press.' The amendment is narrowly drawn, which is why it is more often referred to than quoted: it says nothing about the freedom to make money by broadcasting rubbish, which is the sense in which broadcasters sometimes understand it.

But that is not in question in the coverage of current events. There the fear is that by suppressing unfavourable news and opinion, a government could clear the way for its own propaganda. That fear has been at least as real in many twentieth-century American minds as it was when the Bill of Rights was drawn up.

The FCC, the arm of government in broadcasting, was made deliberately weak when it was established in 1934 by the Communications Act. 'Nothing in this act shall be understood or construed to give the Commission the power of censorship over the radio communications or signals transmitted by any radio station, and no regulation or condition shall be promulgated or fixed by the Commission which shall interfere with the right of free speech by means of radio communication.'[1] For long periods the Commission itself, in the sense of a majority of the seven commissioners, has appeared to hold that this limited its writ to handing out call letters and seeing that transmission towers were properly painted: it could exert no influence over what was said or sung on the air. The broadcasting industry has wholeheartedly agreed.

But the Commission was also given the crucial power of issuing or withholding licences. Ever since 1934 there has been intermittent argument, in the courts and out of them, about whether a licence should depend simply on a station's technical performance or on the quality of its programmes as well. During a bold period in 1946 the FCC itself pointed out in a 'blue book' that broadcasters could in fact afford to carry more unsponsored material of public interest than they did, to originate more material locally instead of taking it from the networks or the record companies, and to broadcast fewer advertisements.[2] The industry protested, and the point was not pressed. Another attempt at regulating programmes was made in 1960, not long after the fuss about cheating in quiz shows, and another seemed in preparation late in 1968; but still the FCC had recourse very sparingly to their power of not renewing licences. Stations lost their licences from time to time for being unpunctual in getting on the air or for running treasure hunts without treasure, but never for putting on trivial programmes, and hardly ever for putting on pernicious programmes. A South Carolina radio station was refused renewal in March 1963 on the grounds, among others, that it had broadcast dirty programmes; but in June 1966 the Commission renewed the licence of a suburban Los Angeles radio station which the Anti-Defamation League said had broadcast anti-semitism, and in June 1968 they renewed the licence of a Mississippi television station which two of the Commission's own members described as 'blatantly racist'.

If that is the price of freedom of speech, it is a price that most Americans would probably think worth paying. In the same way, many Americans still regard the freedom to trade as one likes as a natural right; and if, for a station owner or a network, that means freedom to re-run old episodes of *The Beverly Hillbillies*, then that too must be borne with. Station owners tend to defend this second freedom in terms more appropriate to the first, deploying words like 'censorship' when a quiz game is frowned on; and the FCC are so anxious to avoid even the suspicion of censorship that they accept this wide definition of it.

The fact seems to be that the FCC came to regulate the broadcasting industry and stayed to represent it. They became the industry's ambassador to the government instead of the other way round. Relations between regulator and regulated sometimes became embarrassingly close. In March 1960 the then chairman of the Commission acknowledged to a House subcommittee that he had spent six nights on a yacht belonging to the head of a chain of broadcasting stations, and accepted a free ride in his aeroplane. Press comment and the imminence of an election campaign made President Eisenhower, ordinarily a quietist in these as in other matters, press him to resign; and when snow in the Maryland suburbs of Washington threatened to keep the chairman safe at home, the White House sent a car with chains on the tyres to get him to his office so that he could write his letter of resignation.

The Commission might have done more if it had been more encouraged by Congress: changes in broadcasting rules need congressional approval, through the commerce committees of both houses. But the last thing members of Congress want is an uncomfortable relationship with the owners of the local broadcasting stations whose services they need at election time; and for members of the House of Representatives, at least, election time comes round every two years. They are therefore very sensitive to the sensitivities of station owners.

Some of them, in addition, are station owners themselves. On a count made in January 1968 from FCC records, five senators and ten representatives had a personal or family interest in one or more broadcasting stations.[3] Until 1966 the chairmen of both the Senate and the House Commerce Committees had television interests.[4] The investment was an understandable one: television is one of the very few industries that regularly gives a return of about 100 per cent each year on the written-down value of invested capital.

The most notable family interest in American broadcasting is the Johnson family's. In January 1943, when Lyndon Johnson had already been a congressman for nearly six years, his wife bought a rundown radio station in the capital of Texas: KTBC, Austin. (K for an operation west of the Mississippi, on the FCC's rule of thumb: TBC for the Texas Broadcasting Corporation.) Mrs Johnson paid $17,500 for it: she had inherited a little more than that from her mother. The FCC allowed the Johnsons to extend the broadcasting hours without limit and quadruple the transmitting power. CBS took the station on as an affiliate. The Johnsons' profits were invested in farming and banking. By 1948, when Congressman Johnson won his senate seat at the second attempt, his family possessions were worth a million dollars. By 1968, with the only VHF television channel granted by the FCC to Austin, links to all three networks, and other broadcasting ventures in the South-West, the Johnson broadcast holdings alone were valued at ten times that.[5]

Austin is a city of nearly two hundred thousand people. The only other station there was KHFI, transmitting on an ultra-high frequency, which even in the late sixties not all sets could receive. Its managers complained constantly that they were the victims of discrimination: that the networks denied them the opportunity to screen big football games, or that the FCC were slow in dealing with their affairs. In fact Lyndon Johnson took no part in the running of KTBC after 1948; and as soon as he became president in November 1963 a trust was formed for the holdings of his wife and two daughters, who were by then joint owners. But Patrick Nugent, who married the younger daughter Luci in August 1966, went to work for the station on the management side until he returned to the Air Force in March 1968; and FCC officials were aware that rulings which affected the earnings of broadcasting companies in general or of the LBJ Company in particular would be reflected in the personal wealth of a man whose goodwill they preferred to retain.

In a speech in Boston in February 1968 Governor George Romney of Michigan complained that President Johnson had built 'his greatest fortune by having a monopoly position in the radio and television field in his home area. He has obviously benefited from his influence in having such a monopoly position.' If the Governor was serving notice that this would be a campaign issue, the prediction went astray. Within five weeks both he and the President had withdrawn from the contest.

These are some of the checks, arising out of law and custom, on the FCC's exercise of governmental authority over broadcasters. The countervailing balances, the instruments which enable the FCC as the constitutional arm of government in broadcasting to control or influence what is said or shown on the air, are less weighty. They are no more than declarations that if a station airs one side of a controversial question, it should give opportunity for the airing of another side. They go by the name of the fairness doctrine and the personal attack principle. They serve much the same office as the equal opportunities doctrine does, without being limited to election times; and they represent an edifice laboriously constructed on the same few lines of federal law.[6]

This is to say that before the FCC can attempt to compel the broadcasting of a certain fact or opinion, some contrary fact or opinion must have been broadcast. Even at that the industry steadily contests the two principles. The administration have sometimes made use of the fairness doctrine to arrange for a reply at cabinet level to some programme they disliked; but in general these are clumsy and haphazard channels for government propaganda.

In America the theoretical justification of this deliberate weakness of the executive in face of the broadcasting interests rests on the public's right to know. 'It is this right of the public to be informed,' said the FCC in 1949 when they promulgated the fairness doctrine, 'rather than any right on the part of the government, any broadcast licensee or any individual member of the public to broadcast his own particular views on any matter which is the foundation stone of the American system of broadcasting.'[7]

In Britain, on the other hand, the right of the government to broadcast its own particular views is entrenched. It is not heavily used, but it is there. The Independent Television Authority, which stands in something of the same relation to commercial broadcasters in Britain as the FCC does in America, is obliged by law to get the stations under its control to broadcast or not to broadcast whatever any government minister tells it to. It has the legal power to enforce this on the fourteen programme companies who each operate in a different area of the United Kingdom, together with one in the Channel Islands. Besides this it has a legal duty to see that the programmes which go out in its name are inoffensive and on the whole impartial.[8] Its ultimate sanction over its broadcasters, like the FCC's, is the removal of the broadcasting franchise; and in June 1967 it surprised some of them by exercising it. In a general redistribution two companies were forcibly merged and diminished in activity, one had its territory halved and one, Television Wales and the West, had its licence taken away altogether, though not for any political transgression. The only people more astonished than the TWW directors were the FCC commissioners in Washington.

The BBC is under exactly the same obligation, ratified by Parliament, to broadcast or withhold anything the government asks. Should it forget this, the government may take possession of its stations, revoke its licence and dismiss its governors.[9] No wonder Lord Beveridge's committee on broadcasting said in January 1951: 'The formal power of the Government of the day over the British Broadcasting Corporation is absolute.'[10]

Yet this formal power has never been put to major use, and perhaps could not be. Sir Anthony Eden, as Prime Minister at the time of the Franco-British invasion of Suez in October 1956, is said by Harman Grisewood (who was then the BBC Director-General's chief assistant) to have 'instructed the Lord Chancellor to prepare an instrument which would take over the BBC altogether and subject it wholly to the will of the Government'.[11] The Prime Minister believed that the BBC, in giving a voice to dissenting views, was subverting what ought to have been a national war effort. The people who advised him to try a take-over cannot have felt that the government's existing hold over the BBC was as strong as it looked; and in fact the BBC was able to stand by its governors' decision that it should go on behaving as it always had.

Even the right of ministers to broadcast when they want to has been sparingly used. After Labour came to power in October 1964 these ministerial broadcasts on television ran at about the rate of four a year, mostly from the Prime Minister.[12]

Explicit directions were sometimes given to the BBC's external services, which were subject to the same controls as its domestic operations:[13] after the Rhodesian government declared its independence in November 1965, the BBC increased the hours and the signal strength of its services to Central Africa at the British government's request. But inside Britain the legal power remained a reserve power. In their white paper on broadcasting in December 1966, the Wilson government wrote: 'The principle that the public corporations should be independent of the Government has been upheld by successive Administrations since the beginning of broadcasting in the United Kingdom. The Government adhere to this concept.'[14]

When successive postmasters general, as ministers responsible for broadcasting, were asked in the House of Commons to take action against some programme on the grounds that it was disrespectful to the Deity or the Queen or the national prestige, they regularly replied that that was the business of the governors of the BBC and the members of the ITA. Since these people, a dozen on each side, forming the ultimate governing bodies of both organisations, could be appointed and dismissed at will by the government, this might have seemed simply a more covert means to governmental control. Yet as such it would have been so unwieldy as to be unusable. The members of these governing bodies represented the great mass of viewers and listeners with special efficiency in one respect: they seldom agreed. Indeed, they were chosen for their diversity of opinion. Yet in order to take decisions they had to agree. In principle they had the same power over their organisations as a minister had over his department; but at least one former member of the BBC's board of governors, Lady Wootton, noticed that the limitations of collectivity made the board 'more easily dominated by its officials than is any but the weakest Minister by his Civil Servants'.[15]

The anonymous author of the Beveridge report was well aware that BBC officials had not arrived at this point by accident. BBC doctrine, he wrote, 'appears designed to make the Governors resemble the cloud in Wordsworth's poem

> ... that heareth not the loud winds when they call,
> And moveth altogether if it move at all'.[16]

He did not italicise the last five words. The point was clear enough. A professional broadcasting organisation could outmanœuvre a body of ill-assorted amateurs any day.

Governing bodies, like the rest of the constitutional structure of British and American broadcasting, are not a means through which governments can effectively coerce broadcasters.

12 The Voluntary Principle

In both the United States and Britain, such formal powers as the government has over broadcasters are virtually unused. Yet there are ways in which, without recourse to formal powers, a government can have its will of broadcasters none the less. These ways need not be exaggerated: it would be difficult to demonstrate that they had ever resulted in a major injustice or a major alteration to the course of events: but it is useful that they should be understood.

Although in Britain the governors of the BBC and the members of the ITA are hobbled by their numbers and by their distance from the detailed work of their organisations, they have chairmen: men whose formal authority is supreme and who may occasionally exercise it.

In both concerns these chairmen, who commonly serve about five years, have been men of unreproached impartiality. Yet where disputes have arisen between government and broadcasters, their influence has more often than not been exerted on the side of government. This is not out of political sympathy: their political sympathies have often lain away from the government of the day. It is a matter of professional sympathy. As professional politicians and administrators before they came to the job, they have understood government's problems better than other people's.

In November 1950 the BBC chairman, Lord Simon of Wythenshawe, prevailed on the BBC television drama people to cancel a second performance of Val Gielgud's play *Party Manners*. It was another political play about a butler: a Labour cabinet minister recruited one from the impoverished peerage. The play was performed at a time when the second Attlee government had a narrow majority in the Commons. The cancellation was by any test an unwise move. The play had been seen once, so that it was already in the public domain: the audience for a second showing would not have been enormous: cancellation helped the play to new prominence and three months in a West End theatre; and the whole episode increased the feeling that the government was on the run. But Lord Simon had been in local, national and university government all his life, and when the point was put to him he thought it best to spare the government what he considered an unworthy embarrassment.

In October 1965 Ian Smith was in London as Prime Minister of Rhodesia to discuss terms that might prevent him declaring his country's independence. In an interview on Rediffusion's *This Week* for ITV he gave a plausible account of his beliefs. The BBC's *24 Hours* suggested that he should be interviewed on their programme. Lord Normanbrook, the then chairman, became aware that the government were unhappy at the prospect of a further public appeal against their policy, and he arranged that the invitation should not be confirmed. He was within his rights. Yet the chief result was to create more sympathy for Mr Smith than he would have got by setting out his beliefs in a lengthy broadcast, and to give the Rhodesians an excuse to keep Mr Wilson off the air when he went to Salisbury later the same month. Lord Normanbrook had been appointed under a Conservative government; but his training as secretary to the cabinet for nine years made him responsive to any government's suggestion that orderliness in international negotiation was more important than the forms of free discussion.

Lord Normanbrook had never been an elected politician, and Lord Simon of Wythenshawe had never risen beyond the rank of parliamentary secretary to the Ministry of Health. Chairmen's sympathies with government became a matter of renewed discussion in September 1967, when the chairmanship of both broadcasting bodies was taken over by men who had been cabinet ministers. Lord Hill, who had been a cabinet minister in the Macmillan government until July 1962, was moved from the ITA to the BBC; and in at the ITA came Lord Aylestone, who as Herbert Bowden had been a senior member of two Labour governments since October 1964. Within three months Lord Aylestone found himself defending himself and Lord Hill at a lunch in London where they were both guests. 'Our crime apparently is that we are ex-politicians', he said. On the same day, in Glasgow, the joint managing director of Granada Television, Denis Forman, explained and delimited the disquiet which this caused. 'Neither of these noble lords has shown nor will show the slightest inclination to allow his background as a

professional politician to influence him in the way he discharges his
duties. Yet nevertheless television is becoming linked, by way of an
old boy network, to Westminster.'

Opinion at the BBC was particularly jarred by the appointment of
Lord Hill. He was in fact an old BBC hand, having been their
medical man to millions for some years before he went into Parliament in 1950; but his instant translation from the ITA, without the
lapse of a day between, seemed to some BBC men a sharp reminder
from the government that its powers were absolute: it could do anything it liked with the BBC. Robert Lusty, a publisher who was acting chairman at the time, said later in an interview with *The Times*
that the appointment was a strange and unreasonable one which
illustrated 'the total inability of government to recognise the differing natures and conceptions of the BBC and the ITA'.[1]

The system is effective for protecting the citizen as viewer against
the broadcasters. The regulatory influences which these chairmen
lead and represent see to it that he is as far as possible shown honest
news, not shown dishonest advertisements, and so on. The question
is whether the citizen is equally well protected against the government. Where there is a conflict of interest between viewer and
government over what facts or opinions should be disclosed, whose
interest will prevail?

One or two other persuasions work on the government's side.
There is the natural anxiety to keep out of trouble. No reporter is so
dead to human feeling that he escapes it altogether. French reporters, particularly for the ORTF, know the phenomenon so well
that they have a word for it: *autocensure*: every man his own censor.
In Britain it is not so much a matter of omission as of addition, to
make sure that the report is even-handed – that it includes the government's answer as well as the opposition's charge. And this is as it
should be; as long as the facts themselves are somewhere near even-
handed. The problem comes when they are not. During the first half
of 1964, the Conservative government consistently got the worst of
it in the Commons: in strategy, at question-time and in debate.
They knew it themselves. The problem for a reporter in the gallery
was whether to balance his account of this state of affairs or to try
and report it as it was. It was a choice between seeming impartial
and trying to be impartial. The first course would be defensible to all
comers: the second would undoubtedly draw down charges of sub-

jectivism and bias. The first course usually won. Opposition speeches were cut down to leave the same amount of room for the government: ministerial replies had their syntax put right and the scepticism of their reception muted.

Newspaper reporters working for proprietors with firm political views have these problems too. But the pressure to seem fair is particularly acute in television. Television reporters, like all employees, need the goodwill of their employers. But their employers need the goodwill of the government. The BBC need it if they are to get more income from licence fees: independent television companies need it if the rate of tax on their advertisement earnings is not to be increased. Both organisations need it for the grant of new channels, and longer broadcasting hours, and more transmissions in colour. Good relations with government are a condition of continued life. In consequence, television reporters who imperil those relations will not be long in enjoyment of their employers' favour or even of their jobs.

Political reporters on television have other barometers to watch besides their employers. Their work brings them into repeated contact with exactly those sources of power which are most important to their organisations. If they stray into difficulties, they can foresee their own fall before their employers can.

Although the minister responsible for broadcasting is the postmaster-general, no prime minister will now be able to forgo a close interest in it. His job depends on television too much. Since British politics moved in the summer of 1963 into a period where an election was almost permanently imminent, it has become a commonplace for the henchmen of prime ministers and leaders of the opposition to bring pressure to bear on the people who report politics for television. There is nothing discreditable about this pressure: it takes the form of a suggestion that a certain pronouncement should be taken seriously, or a regret that it was not taken seriously, or a complaint that some counter-pronouncement was taken more seriously. Except at times of stress, as when it became clear that the result of the October 1964 election would be very close, the approach is courteous and even cordial and it can be put aside in the same spirit.

The changing factor in television politics is that the men above these figures, politicians at the highest levels, have lived with television for so long that they know exactly which buttons to press. And from where they are they can reach them.

One very simple method, if something said on the air has not found favour, is the call for a transcript. This is not done at the lowly level of press officer to journalist or producer concerned: the private office puts in a call to the office of the chairman of the BBC or the ITA. By this means every level through which the request filters down is made aware of the journalist's imputed transgression. When the transcript comes back – all clean and shining, very different from the grubby notes from which the journalist was actually reading on the air – nothing more happens. Notice has been served.

More serious is the last-minute blackball: the refusal to appear on a programme unless a certain reporter or a certain piece of reporting is removed from it. Sometimes the blackball sticks and the reporter goes: sometimes a compromise is reached. But the havoc caused by the prospect of a huge hole in an important programme is such that few reporters could expect to occasion it more than once and survive.

Most serious is the calculated withdrawal of co-operation at a moment that will produce maximum mortification. Of this the classic instance was Mr Wilson's refusal in April 1966, as he returned in triumph from Liverpool to London after a general election victory that seemed to confirm him in power for ever, to give the BBC an interview which would have been the first live transmission from a train. This was not a move against the BBC reporter on the train, John Morgan: it was a reply to what the Prime Minister considered a series of affronts in the Corporation's political coverage. The pith of his private complaints was that the BBC had not been treating the Labour government like a real government. They gave the Conservative opposition the right of reply to ministerial broadcasts in circumstances, he believed, where they would not have given it to a Labour opposition: they pursued the Prime Minister for an election debate with the Leader of the Opposition long past the point where they had ceased to pursue the Conservative prime minister at the election before; and they blandly assumed that the Prime Minister would be a guinea-pig for their miracle of railway television. He decided not to be.

It was a carefully limited show of strength, using the advantages of surprise. He had considered denying the BBC an interview the night before as well, in a school in his constituency at Huyton where his own votes were counted; but he thought it better not to, and John Morgan and I interviewed him together.

A few hours later the railway porters clapped as the breakfast-time train pulled out of Liverpool Lime Street station for London. On the front end was an entire coach made over to the BBC. One compartment was fitted up as a studio, another as a control room, the luggage-van as a recording room. Beside the videotape machine stood the transmitting equipment, which spilled over into the driver's cab. The equipment could only transmit on a certain stretch of line in Buckinghamshire, where receiving gear had been set up on a hill overlooking the track. This was explained to the Prime Minister: the BBC would like him to do the interview somewhere near Bletchley. Only then did they learn, from a member of his staff, that he would not be doing the interview anywhere.

To point his refusal, he gave me an interview in the next compartment to his own with every appearance of equanimity. This ITV interview was not live, but it was shot with an electronic camera and successfully videotaped. The tape was put off the train at Crewe and screened twenty minutes later.

Later in the day the Prime Minister was asked why he had not given a second interview, for the BBC. 'I was tired after the first one', he said.

British television journalists can find grounds for comfort or alarm, as they choose, in the corresponding situation at the White House. Comfort, because there are stages in the covert influencing of television which have not been approached in Britain: alarm, because fashions in guiding public opinion have a way of crossing the Atlantic sooner or later.

As head of state as well as chief executive, and with no established leader of the opposition to dispute his primacy except for four or five months in every four years, the president is in a very strong position to get what he wants from television. He is a fount of favours. If he is opposed to legislation which would have the networks licensed and so potentially inconvenienced by the FCC, or to systems of toll television which would increase competition, then the industry needs no other protector. He is also a fount of news. Journalists find the White House, as the chief source of proposals for legislative action at home and for martial or diplomatic action abroad, incomparably the most interesting place in the country.

In consequence, if the president wants television coverage he can have it; and if he wants television coverage of a certain kind, he stands a good chance of having it.

Soon after he came to power, President Johnson developed great punctilio about not allowing his staff to ask for television time in so many words. They would use instead the phrase that a certain speech or press conference was 'available for live coverage'. It made little difference. The network representatives in Washington could read the signal.

What they could not know was whether the utterance would be presidential or partisan; or the second believing itself to be the first. In December 1967 the networks were alerted to a speech at Miami Beach which would be an important statement on foreign and domestic policy – a speech they would not want to miss. The electronic cameras were wheeled out. The speech turned out to be only notable for an attack on the Republicans in Congress: they were called 'wooden soldiers of the status quo', nay-sayers, an old buggy that could only go backwards and downhill. The networks were obliged to consume more time on politics by giving the Republicans the right of reply.

In much the same way President Johnson could without effort get television time for his lieutenants. In February 1968 he floated the notion to network reporters, in an afternoon gathering of journalists at the White House, that their employers ought to provide Mr Rusk and Mr McNamara with an hour of television time for discussion of current issues. This was just after the successful Vietcong offensive at the time of the Vietnamese new year, when Communists briefly occupied several towns and part of the American embassy in Saigon. By eleven o'clock the same evening, NBC were able to announce that Mr Rusk and Mr McNamara would appear on a special sixty-minute edition of *Meet the Press* in two days' time.

There was some argument about whether the fact that the four newspapermen-questioners had been approved by the White House meant that the President was dictating the shape of the programme. Senator Fulbright, who was put out because his Senate Foreign Relations Committee had not at that time been able to persuade Mr Rusk to answer its questions in public, described such programmes as 'more or less controlled exhibitions'; and added that the man who ran the programme, Lawrence Spivak, knew he would be dropped from the list of favoured programmers if the questions were too tough.

In fact the questions were neither too tough nor too submissive, and Mr Rusk gave an efficient Secretary of State's performance, not allowing that there was anything more than 'grumpiness' among the South Vietnamese. The broadcast's value to the administration was only impaired by the fact that Mr McNamara was within a month of leaving his job as Secretary of Defence and could not altogether keep down his release-happiness. He conceded that things might have been done differently in Vietnam, and that mistakes had been made; and he quoted four lines from T. S. Eliot's *Little Gidding* which his wife had pointed out to him:

> We shall not cease from exploration
> And the end of all our exploring
> Will be to arrive where we started
> And know the place for the first time.

President Johnson could not merely secure coverage: he could influence the form it took. When he gave three network reporters a shared interview in his oval office at the White House in December 1967, there were two pauses during which he watched an immediate videotape recording of what he had already said, discussed it, and considered what should be said next. It took two and a half hours to produce eighty minutes' worth of videotape; and his presence was felt in the process of removing another twenty-two minutes' worth to get the programme down to length. The editing was done by a network committee in New York, on a precedent established in similar circumstances for President Kennedy. It had been agreed that the White House should have a veto on material held damaging to national security. President Johnson left that evening for Canberra on what turned into a journey round the world. He took with him not merely a transcript of what he had said but an actual videotape – a reel two inches thick and eighteen across. The presidential Boeing, Air Force One, was equipped to run it through for him. The suggestions that he repeatedly radioed back were not all concerned with national security.

These are pressures on institutions. Pressures on individuals can be at least as formidable. The minor rewards and punishments in the gift of a head of state are themselves not inconsiderable. The chat with the president in his office: the invitation to a state dinner, with the reporter's wife asked too, to show her that her husband really does mingle with the mighty: the arm thrown carelessly round the shoulder at the president's country place – these are all rewards; and their selective withholding is a punishment.

There are other punishments which touch a journalist more closely. A regular White House correspondent who stood up to ask questions at presidential press conferences and was regularly ignored in favour of other questioners would be aware that this was not accidental. He could survive it. But if the White House staff also refused to answer his questions, by dint of being unavailable when he rang and not returning his call, he would find his work difficult to do.

The telephone is a powerful disciplinary instrument in other ways. A telephone call from the head of state is something that no private citizen can take with total insouciance. President Johnson sometimes spent twenty minutes on the telephone straightening out a single reporter. He was not the first president to resort to the direct approach: President Kennedy used it too. But President Kennedy seems to have believed more in the expiatory value of punishment. 'If Kennedy didn't like a story you'd done', a senior Washington newspaperman once said, 'he might chew you out, and that would be it. If you offend Johnson, he'll never, never, never forgive you: at least, not unless you roll over on your back and put your legs in the air ever afterwards. And the word goes to his staff too.'

All these considerations apply to journalists who use the written as well as the spoken word. In November 1967 and again in April 1968 the Johnson administration was charged by professional newspaper bodies with organising 'a White House snow job'. But it was a White House television reporter who said: 'This man would like to have the kind of control over the information services that Goebbels had.'

A television reporter is more vulnerable to presidential displeasure than a newspaperman, because he cannot cover events retrospectively: if the word that the president is making a sudden journey is withheld from him, he cannot make arrangements that the journey should be filmed. One or two incidents like that and he will have to change his style of reporting or his job. Again, the unannounced press conference as evolved by President Johnson is especially difficult for television. The word comes over the loudspeaker in the west lobby that the president will see the press in his office now. Very few but the White House regulars will be there to hear it, and that is the point: the experts, the big guns, are kept away. Television is also kept away, by design: not the reporters, but the camera crews. Even if the camera is loaded, the whole rigmarole of lighting and focusing and running out a microphone lead cannot be got through in time. Television can do nothing at the White House except by permission.

President Johnson was always a close student of television. From early in his presidency he had three sets in his bedroom, one tuned to each of the three network stations in Washington. NBC's *Today* show was an unvarying part of his morning routine. He watched as many of the network news shows as he could. And his interest was in the performers as much as in the news they delivered. He had a politician's eye for their rise and fall. If a Washington reporter disappeared from the screen, he would check to discover whether the man was on holiday, on assignment or on the slide; and he would adjust his attitude accordingly. If a man appeared less often, he would enjoy marks of presidential favour less often: he had less to offer in return.

But President Johnson would also attend to what they said on the air; and if he disliked it, there were grades of correction. There was the summons to his office for sorrowful rebuke. There was the word from the press secretary to the local bureau chief. As the weapon of last resort there was the word from the President to the network chief – with whom he might well have personal as well as business links.

This was an artillery that no reporter could hope to withstand. If an American president chooses to see his relations with television as war, then it is one war he can win.

President Johnson may have outdistanced British politicians in these techniques, but he remained a moderate in relation to what might have been.

In a television interview broadcast in September 1967, Barry Goldwater said that at the Republican convention in San Francisco in July 1964 'we had every cable of every television company and every radio company marked up in the loft of the Cow Palace. If anybody got a little too obnoxious to us, they would always have cable trouble.'

The interview went out over the educational network. The next day Mr Goldwater said he had been joking. 'There never was any thought of cutting lines.'

No one was quite sure. In the words of one of the campaign slogans that undid him – it was printed across a mushroom cloud on the placards – 'In your heart you know he might'.

PART V

Television and Results

13 Watch and Vote

The laws that politicians have made about television, and the habits they have developed towards it, are a recognition that television is a political force. What politicians still do not know in any detail is how much of a force it is.

In democratic countries, the established test of a political force is the ballot-box or the voting-machine. It may be an imperfect one, but it is the plainest, and the only one that politicians are interested in. Its weakness as a measuring instrument is that a vote is seldom simple: voters are prompted by several sources of information to choose between groups of people each offering whole collections of ideas, and it is seldom possible to be sure which elements in each grouping were the persuaders. More specifically, enquirers have found it difficult to separate and quantify the effect of evidence supplied by television.

They have found it difficult even in cases where television can be isolated as by far the leading source of information in the circumstances under study. There is the simple instance of the American west coast vote. Because Eastern Time is three hours ahead of Pacific Time (and six hours ahead of the time in western Alaska, with stages in between), and because communities in the East begin closing their polls and producing indicative results at six in the evening or even earlier, and because most people across the country go to vote in the evening, it happens that a great many people vote in the West with some notion of which way the votes are going. This they get from television, with a little help from radio. It has never been clear what effect the notion has; or even that it has any effect at all.

The President of CBS, Frank Stanton, repeatedly suggested before the 1968 elections that polling day should last twenty-four hours, the same twenty-four hours everywhere; which would lift from broadcasting the odium of seeming partial to one side at the very end of the campaign after it had struggled so hard to be impartial throughout it. Dr Stanton dismissed as 'unsupported speculations' any ideas that the advance information changed votes. But American politicians long believed that it did. President Eisenhower believed it: on polling day in 1960, at eight o'clock in the evening, Washington time, he went on television to counter the effect he expected on the west coast from what then appeared to be a Kennedy landslide. And in the end California went the other way by a very narrow margin.

There was no good evidence available on whether the Republicans won in California because they were roused by the General, or stung by the prospect of a Democratic victory, or reinforced by Democrats who sympathised with an apparent underdog, or helped by complacent Democratic abstention. But a number of academics got their heads down over the problem in the interval before the next presidential election. So did a number of politicians. The politicians' labours resulted in at least six bills which would in various ways have prevented the broadcasting of results or predictions before all polls were closed. None of them became law. The academics produced at least seven research studies of 1964 polling, all of them considered by a senate subcommittee.[1] Two of them were paid for by CBS, and one by ABC. That was the year when President Johnson won all but six states. The researchers all concluded that there was no evidence, or very little, of either what they called a bandwagon effect or an underdog effect; though two of them thought there was at least a possibility that some voters had been influenced to stay away, and there was general agreement that more work would have to be done.

If it has been difficult to find the effect of television on voting where it is clearly the dominant force in the field, it is not surprising that scholars have found it even more difficult to detect its impact on voting at large. It has been considered together with other channels of information in much American research; where 'a number of studies, some performed in the laboratory and some in the social world, indicate that persuasive mass communication functions far more frequently as an agent of reinforcement than as an agent of change'.[2] In other words, except in areas where they have no opinions to start with, people are much more likely to be convinced than converted by television and its fellows. A study of the response to the Kennedy-Nixon debates found that television crystallised attitudes rather than altering them.[3] Another political scientist wrote: 'It is safe to conclude that the major influence of the media upon political attitudes is by and large a reinforcement of the status quo.'⁴ Few groups, as well as few individuals, are likely to suffer an actual change of mind as they watch.

The point was underlined by the findings of the BBC's audience research department at the 1964 and 1966 general elections in Britain. Of the sound and television broadcasts sponsored by the political parties in 1964, they discovered that most people only found persuasive what they were disposed to agree with. 'Each broadcast tended to be rated as more interesting, more reliable and even better presented by those who supported the sponsoring party than by those who opposed it.'⁵ And the same finding was reproduced in exactly the same words in their 1966 report.

There are politicians who are aware of this limit to television's reach. But elections still have to be won; and since practical electioneering is still a largely haphazard business, where the candidate throws assorted seed about with no knowledge of which grain will grow and which will not, he has to use as many of the available means as he can, from bumper-stickers to sky-writing. There could be no question of leaving television off the list.

American candidates have been taking their television advertising increasingly in spots: announcements lasting between ten seconds and a minute, with some of five minutes. In 1960, during the campaign itself, the two presidential candidates used 9060 spot announcements: in 1964 they used 29,300. In 1962, the total recorded for all candidates in the general election campaign was 94,009: in 1966, the next off-year, it had gone up to 154,398; while the number of hours devoted to paid politics at greater length went down from 2399 to 2110.⁶

Campaign managers liked spots because they seemed to offer more for the money: although they were proportionately more expensive than longer periods of time, they came at the viewer more often and gave him less occasion to switch off. Advertising men liked them because they demanded technical ingenuity. Politicians liked them, particularly the short ones, because they avoided the notorious danger of banishing or curtailing a favoured programme. In 1956, when the Democrats had taken no more than five minutes of the most favoured of all, Adlai Stevenson got a telegram which read: 'I like Ike, and I love Lucy: drop dead.'⁷

On the other hand, there were complaints that such short announcements reduced television to an electronic billboard: that they debased discussion instead of informing it. Some of the spots used by the Democrats in the 1964 presidential campaign were thought so sensational by the Democrats themselves that they were suppressed. They were made by a New York advertising agency, Doyle Dane Bernbach, which also worked on Mr Humphrey's pre-convention campaign in 1968. Two of the 1964 spots made graphic play of the contrast between the idyllic Johnson present and a phantasmagoric Goldwater future: a little girl pulling petals off a daisy, with her count cross-faded into the countdown for a nuclear blast: a little girl licking an ice-cream cone, with a woman's voice explaining about strontium-90 and Senator Goldwater's opposition to a test-ban treaty. Both were only shown once. Another one, which simply showed a hand reaching for what was supposed to be the nuclear button, also had a short run. But the one which showed a pair of hands tearing up a social security card was repeated many times. Republicans believed that they were all powerfully and unfairly effective.

Another New York agency, Jack Tinker and Partners, did comparable work for Nelson Rockefeller when he successfully defended the New York governorship in 1966. The agency themselves regarded the campaign as the clearest possible evidence of the vote-getting power of television. When they took their client over, he was almost four-to-one down in the opinion polls. Since they thought he was an indifferent television performer they decided, they said afterwards, not to run the candidate: they would run his record. One of their advertisements was a dialogue with a fish about the Governor's labours against polluted water: another was an account of his achievements as a road-builder, over a close-up of white lane-markings clicking past under the camera. There were six more.[8] The Governor won by nearly 400,000 votes.

It may have been television that did it: alternatively, it may have been the general anti-Democratic movement after three years of President Johnson. It may have been the hiring of professional television people; though in 1960 the Kennedy staff men believed that television efforts worsened after the professionals moved in, because they had to have the issues explained to them. Few things about television are susceptible of proof.

*

In Britain in 1966 the one-minute political commercial had not yet arrived. The only overt method of broadcast political proselytising allowed was still the party political broadcast: ten or fifteen minutes on television, mostly in the studio, with sparse and predictable film – political meetings, happy schoolchildren, unhappy workers. Attempts at anything that savoured of high-pressure persuasion were frowned on. In August 1964, just before the general election of that year, the Conservatives had experimented with a short film about a wife who suddenly came to the view, when her husband bought a new car, that his Labour convictions were out of date. (Wife: 'We haven't done so bad. Got a house of our own, a car, the kid goes to a decent school, nobody's going short, it's not so bad.' Husband: 'That's not the point.' Wife: 'Oh, that is the point. That's the whole point of all this election business. We're doing all right.'[9]) The film had been made by a London agency, Colman Prentis and Varley. A number of people were worried by the overt suggestion that voters chose political allegiances as they chose soap powders, by results. None of the parties renewed the attempt in 1966.

The original agreement on party political broadcasts was made in 1939 between the three main parties and the BBC, and it was codified in February 1947 in a document which is long since out of print.[10] The 1954 Television Act admitted ITV to the privilege of transmitting the broadcasts, and the passage of time secured for the minor parties a share in making them. The Welsh and Scottish Nationalists had five minutes each on Welsh and Scottish television in the 1964 election; and the Communists joined them with five minutes of national time in 1966.

But the bulk of the allotted time remained with the major parties. In the 1966 campaign the Labour party and the Conservatives had an hour each, and the Liberals thirty-five minutes. No measure can exist of whether the broadcasts did what the parties hoped from them. They had every chance of being effective, in that for the constant viewer they were inescapable. They went out at exactly the same times on both BBC channels and on ITV. This was dignified into the principle of simultaneity. What it meant was that no channel was going to risk having its viewers look for something different on another channel: they might learn dangerous new habits.

The parties never became popular broadcasters. When the programmes came on, about a seventh of the entire television audience in the country seem to have switched off their sets. The parties' only comfort was that this was a smaller proportion than in 1964, when about a quarter did, or than 1959, when about a fifth did.[11] 70 per cent of the people who answered questions put in November 1967 on a BBC programme, *Talkback*, thought that there was too much of these broadcasts.

None of this disposed the parties to give them up. They liked them for exactly the same reason that television people disliked them: that the broadcasting organisation could not intervene. It was reduced to the level of common carrier. It sent out what was set before it without objection or comment. Yet senior politicians were possessive about these programmes not chiefly because they believed that a programme produced on those terms would be more persuasive. The broadcasts were not looked on as exercises in persuasion. The parties as corporate entities lost control of them to a small group of politicians who looked on them as exercises in self-projection. This was not all selfishness, or concern for their own electoral salvation: politicians would never be able to survive the cruelties of their world without a number of self-delusive vanities, and one vanity prevalent among them is the belief that they are convincing on television.[12]

This kind of broadcast is vested with a special importance by opposition parties, and has contributed in one respect to influencing votes cast for them. It has played a leading part in the tendency of British television to give undeserved prominence in a two-party system to a third party. In 1959 the Liberals won about an eighth of the votes won by their nearest competitor among the major parties, and a forty-third of the Commons seats. Throughout the next five years they nevertheless had about a third of the television time made over to the Conservatives or the Labour party; and in the 1964 general election they had pushed their allowance up to three-fifths. This advantage was not turned into parliamentary seats on any significant scale; but their tally of votes went up to within a quarter of each of their main competitors. More important, they were able to remain a political presence throughout a time when the figures suggested that they had all but disappeared.

Clearly there were other reasons for this besides party political broadcasts. But again, the chief of them was to do with television. Partly because of the influence of the party broadcast system, Liberals were given about the same proportion of space in a much more useful area of television: news programmes. Broadcasters made this distribution because they found it easiest to defend in case of complaint. They also found that Liberals were pleasantly undemanding people to deal with. They had to be: they did not have either the fact of office or the possibility of it at their back. They shamed the broadcasters into giving them a generous share of time by never pressing for it. Or almost never. At a count in a Middlesex school hall at the end of the first Greater London Council elections in April 1964, a vocal group of Liberals protested against the fact that neither of the two local MPs there to offer televised comment was a Liberal. Neither could have been: there were no local Liberal MPs. As the reporter on the spot, I threw the protest out, probably not very politely. The next morning a senior official from Liberal party headquarters telephoned me to apologise for his over-eager partisans.

The other main factor in the maintenance of a Liberal presence was that they used their broadcast time well. Both in their party broadcasts and their news appearances, they were a little more disposed than the spokesmen of other parties to float new ideas and question old ones.

Yet with all this – disproportionate time on television, more than usual skill in filling it – the Liberal vote went down again in 1966. It was a further demonstration that any direct effect of television on voting is very difficult to identify.

The connection, then, between what people see on television and how they decide to vote is at best obscure.

All that can be safely said is that television is a prime provider of the information which helps people decide. Here the academic evidence is plentiful. The Survey Research Center at the University of Michigan found as early as 1956 that television was the leading source of information for their sample of voters. Just under three-quarters had got some information from television, and just under a half had got 'the most information' from it.[13] The Leeds study of the 1959 election in Britain posited among its sample voters in Pudsey and West Leeds a communication barrier through which no persuasion passed, and information only passed as a result of television.[14] Roper poll enquiries concluded that by 1961 television was the American public's most believed source of news, and by 1963 its primary source.[15] Other studies have claimed that among the American Negro poor it becomes virtually a unique source.

Even here, two things are worth remembering. One is that viewers have still found it possible to be deeply sceptical of information offered by television when they are so minded. Rather than believe that they lived in a repressive society, great numbers of Americans at all levels of education were convinced that television pictures of police action in Chicago in August 1968 had been so selective as to be simply untruthful.

Second, in so far as television is an electorate's chief source of information, the needs of a sophisticated democracy are not much advanced. Old problems return. The kind of circumscribed, pictorial information which television can present is not enough to guide voters towards well-based decisions.

14 Screening the Candidates, 1968

It was to be expected that the American election campaign of 1968, since it was fought with passion and great sums of money, should have unprecedented spread on television. Cameras kept watch from the first identifiable moment to the last.

The opening vote of that long electoral season was cast by a New Hampshire surgeon, Dr Elliott Foster. He was moderator of the town meeting at the winter resort of Waterville Valley. When the political year once again began with a New Hampshire primary, his town meeting decided to open the local polls at the first possible moment on the March day appointed: midnight. The polling-place was a nursery school in a wooden hut surrounded by fir-trees and fresh snow.

By half past eleven the twenty-three electors of Waterville Valley were all met. By six minutes to twelve the floor was clear of small desks and the ceiling had sheets hanging from it to make voting-booths. Dr Foster stepped forward to begin the polling.

I stopped him. Would he mind waiting a moment? It was not a scruple about the clock: it was simply that our camera had jammed. He agreed to wait. The jam was quickly cleared, and voting still began before midnight. But it had an authenticity now which transcended legal correctness: it would be safely on television.

American and European television organisations spent more money on the 1968 elections than they had on any previous American campaign. Yet the inadequacies of television as a way of reporting politics were never more clearly set out.

There was general agreement that the heads of the national debate ought to be the Vietnam war, the cities and the economy. But both the problems and the solutions were more easily talked about than shown. The economy was as hard to put into pictures as ever. Governor Rockefeller's advertising agents, the boldest television innovators of the year, tried explaining inflation with a shrinking

picture of a dollar bill and a squeaking sound produced by manipulating an unseen balloon. It was mesmeric, but it was not
enlightening. Both the cities and Vietnam posed special difficulties
for television throughout the summer of 1968. The violent action
in both was interrupted for long periods; and even if it had not been
there were reasons against exhaustive coverage. Slum disturbances
were to be made light of. The word had gone out in the Kerner
riot commission report of the previous March. It was so faithfully
observed that in the suburbs of every large city there were people
who believed that riots were still happening but not being reported
any more. The argument against detailed reports of the fighting in
Vietnam was simpler and more cruel: for all their vividness, they
had ended by capturing with peculiar accuracy the boringness of
war. The only question about the war which interested anybody now
was how to end it. The administration's ideas on that were being
put to the North Vietnamese at the Hotel Majestic in Paris. But
sound cameras were not allowed inside, so the talks quickly became
a bore too. Further, in both areas of conflict, the cities and Vietnam,
the argument was about the future, which was not yet available to
cameras. In sum, television could show little of the central problems
of the election and almost nothing of the solutions being canvassed.

Any electorate, though, spends more time discussing people than
problems; and here television could present the basis for a judgment. Yet almost the whole process of choosing between people was
out of the hands of the electorate. It was as true in 1968 as it had
been in 1911, when that professional cynic Ambrose Bierce compiled *The Devil's Dictionary*, that the right of suffrage was 'the
right to vote for the man of another man's choice'. It was widely
believed that television would at least let everyone know how that
other man's choice was made: how the party regulars chose the
party's candidates. John Lindsay, the Mayor of New York, said
on NBC's *Johnny Carson Show* as the Republicans were gathering
at Miami Beach that television would ensure public decisions. Nothing could have been less true. There were television cameras in
the town in hundreds: on the diving-platforms of hotel swimming
pools, on the roofs of Cadillacs, on huge extending limbs called
cherry-pickers, on the shoulders of sweating cameramen. It would
have been no surprise to see them in the palm-trees. But they were
not on the private yachts in which Mr Nixon's friends took delegates for rides, nor in the hotel sitting-room where Senator Strom

Thurmond and the Reverend Billy Graham helped choose Governor Spiro Agnew as candidate for vice president; and if they had been, the discussion would have been moved somewhere else.

Television incurred a new disability during the campaign. It grew less easy to believe. Even before the deliberate disbelief that greeted the pictures from Chicago, viewers had come nearer the opinion that as a source of first-hand evidence on political fact television might not always be unimpeachable. 1968 was the year when larger sums than ever before were laid out to buy political advertising on television. This advertising always carried at the end, and sometimes at the beginning, an indication that it had been paid for, and by whom. But throughout its length its makers were in most cases at pains to see that it looked as much like news television as possible. It was indistinguishable from a panel interview programme or a filmed report in a news bulletin. Two Rockefeller advertisements shown in the last fortnight before the Republican convention used a 'moving super', a device ordinarily reserved for sudden tidings of great importance. While the pictures showed the Governor's head or a shouting crowd, a ribbon of letters passed horizontally across the screen with a report of rising Rockefeller popularity among influential Republicans or voters in general. NBC only accepted the advertisements after the superimposed words had been changed to move vertically, like the credits at the end of a programme; but CBS showed the advertisements before they asked for the same change, and ABC never asked for it. Many viewers will have seen the horizontal signal, sat up a little straighter in their chairs, realised that they had been deceived, and withdrawn a little more of their trust from television journalism.

The confusion was deepened because remarkably little was reported about these paid programmes, except for occasional guesses at their cost. News organisations that would report a candidate's speech to a hundred people would carry no mention of what he said on paid television to ten million. It is true that the candidate's headquarters were themselves often coy about this material: it was not aimed at journalists, and they did not go out of their way to supply texts or even times. That partly explained newspaper reticence. Television stations may have taken the view that their viewers could see the material for themselves. But by saying almost nothing about these advertisements made in deliberate imitation of their news broadcasts, they allowed the distinction between news and political advertisement to be further blurred.

They also missed one of television's own most significant contributions to the 1968 campaign. In no previous presidential campaign had there been so much paid political television. The Rockefeller use of it to urge his claims on convention delegates was unprecedented. In the primaries it provided the best evidence of a candidate's chosen style and the scale of his effort. It clinched victory and underlined defeat.

Nothing more accurately caught the different tone of the campaigns mounted by George Romney and Richard Nixon than the different use they made of the same bought television opportunity in pursuit of the Republican nomination.

Governor Romney was the first man to get into the 1968 presidential struggle, and the first man to give it up. He came away even before the end of the New Hampshire primary. His last major broadcast as a candidate was an hour's paid 'telethon' in February 1968 from the only commercial television station in New Hampshire – a converted red-brick house at the end of the main street of Manchester, a textile town barely more appealing than the one from which it took its name.

A telethon only differs from any other interview programme in that the questions come not from journalists but from viewers at large, and are therefore notionally more direct. On this occasion telephoned questions were taken down by twelve women and ferried to three questioners: a congressman's wife, a lawyer, and the chaplain to the lower house of the New Hampshire legislature. This was to keep the candidate from becoming bogged in direct altercation with viewers, as had happened to Hubert Humphrey in West Virginia in 1960.[1] But the twelve women had been given the job as a reward for service in the Romney cause, and they had to be seen. In a small studio the Governor was scarcely twenty feet away from them: while he was talking he had constant switchboard chatter in his ears. 'Good evening – this is the *Ask George Romney* programme – may I have your question, please?' 'Can you go a little more slowly, because I don't take shorthand.' 'Are you *Miss* Meadows? Thank you very much, Miss Meadows.' One supporter's telephoned question was simply whether they could keep the noise down.

They were not the only source of noise. Two film crews who had been allowed into the studio talked freely among themselves about the poor sound quality and walked out from time to time to fetch soft drinks. There was also a local anchor-man who would chip in unexpectedly to tell viewers what they were watching.

Governor Romney made head against all this as best he could. Well scrubbed and intent, he looked like a Mormon missionary gone to his reward, with the short hair on either side of his head gleaming like little white wings. 'He is so damned telegenic', said a member of his staff who watched a monitor in the hallway outside. True or not, it was unwise to rely on this quality without any production expertise to back it. In these conditions the Governor could say nothing worth saying, and he was allowed to make an elementary mistake. In line with his belief in personal magnetism, he took it as read that the proper thing to do was to look not towards his questioners but straight into the camera. This in itself seemed discourteous and contrived. But in addition there was no floor manager to show him which was the right camera; so that he often talked for several sentences into the wrong one, while the cameramen gesticulated at him and the viewers saw the side of his head. The whole programme was eloquent of bewilderment.

Two days later a private poll showed that Mr Nixon, the only other candidate on the Republican ballot, could be expected to get 73 per cent of the Republican vote in the state. Within a week Governor Romney had withdrawn his candidacy. Mr Nixon's final score was 78 per cent.

The programme was followed the very next night on the same station by *The Nixon Answer*, a smooth half-hour compilation on videotape from discussions between Mr Nixon and groups of citizens held in the community hall at Hillsboro, New Hampshire, three weeks before. It was a technique which his campaign used again in other states during and after the primaries. But the true comparison with *Ask George Romney* was the only other telethon of the pre-convention campaign. Two days before polling in the Oregon primary at the end of May, television stations covering most of the populated part of the state carried an hour and a half of a production called *Ask Richard Nixon*.

The Nixon people had borrowed the form of the title, and the broad technique; but that was all. They brought in a studio director from Burbank, the television city outside Los Angeles. The studio they used, in Portland, was a large one: large enough to accommodate an audience which included the candidate's wife and his prospective son-in-law David Eisenhower. The twenty telephonists were young and personable. They included the candidate's two daughters, cunningly flanked by two Negro girls. They were also efficient: they took thirteen times as many questions as the matrons of Manchester, though Mr Nixon's rate of two minutes for each answer was no faster than Governor Romney's. Once the programme had begun there was no local announcer to interrupt it. Instead of the three Romney questioners there was only one: Bud Wilkinson, who had once been a football coach and a senatorial candidate in Oklahoma. He put the questions with such an accomplished blend of good fellowship and deference that when he asked who was to be the candidate for vice president Mr Nixon answered: 'Well, by the way you've been asking these questions I'd like you.' Both men laughed quickly, to dispel the thought that this was as good a basis for the choice as any other.

One Nixon advantage turned out to be more apparent than real: his programme was in colour. American colour television, even in the best conditions, could not then muster a skin tone more plausible than bright orange or bright pink. Governor Romney had been better off in black and white.

At the end, which was also the end of his primary campaign, Mr Nixon walked down to the audience and thanked them for thus taking part in the democratic process; but until then he kept his eyes on Mr Wilkinson, which was both tidy and polite, and at the same time sent his answer further afield. 'Miss Elizabeth Young of Klamath Falls wants to know how you keep your weight down.' 'Well, Miss Young, I have two very strong arms, and I use them to push the food away. I don't eat desserts, but I love them. . . . What do I eat? Since I'm in a state that produces a lot of cheese, I eat cheese – cottage cheese. And I put ketchup on it. Then it doesn't taste so bad.'

It was a cheerful and assured performance which reflected a supremely competent campaign. The problem about beard shadow had been smoothed away. Sun-tan was said to be the specific, though make-up helped. All that was left of the Nixon of 1960 was an occasional impulse to say unfounded things if he thought he could get away with them. He was against compulsory medical insurance, he said, because it had reduced the standard of medical care in

Britain – 'and as a result many Britons come to America for treatment'.

Oregon was the television primary. The two million citizens of that remote and rainwashed state were offered a more intensive course of political television than any other group of American voters throughout 1968; and most of it paid for out of campaign funds.

With the campaign squeezed by the primary calendar into a fortnight, there was no other way to cover an area slightly larger than the United Kingdom; and campaigners used television with special vigour because none of the candidates could afford a bad result. It was Mr Nixon's last stand before the Republican convention: Governor Rockefeller's showing had to meet comparison with his victory in Oregon in 1964: Governor Reagan had to do justice to his position as a neighbouring governor. Senator McCarthy needed a majority of the Democratic votes if he was ever to catch Senator Robert Kennedy: Senator Kennedy needed it if he was to keep his magic. (Mr Humphrey was on the ballot only for the vice-presidency.)

But there could be no more than one winner in each party. So when Mr Nixon won handsomely with 73 per cent of the Republican vote, and Senator McCarthy narrowly with 45 per cent of the Democratic vote, three other candidacies were seriously set back. With New Hampshire, which was partly responsible for President Johnson's retirement, Oregon was the most influential of the 1968 primaries.

Governor Rockefeller was the least damaged. His name was not on the Oregon ballot: he had had it withdrawn in the days before he declared his presidential aims explicitly. His partisans in Portland could urge voters to write it in. But they only won the necessary covert encouragement from Rockefeller headquarters in New York eight days before polling; and because of the variety of voting methods used in the state, they had to spend their skill and money on preaching the how rather than the why of a write-in. 'Have you ever written history?' a voice asked in one ten-second message as a hand brought a pen down on a Portland ballot-paper. For Republicans the paper was blue, and the size of a table-cloth: voters had to make nearly seventy other choices too, of local reference. 'Tuesday's your chance', the voice went on. 'Write in Rockefeller.'

The advertisements were made in haste by a Portland agency. The facetiousness of one of them foresaw failure. It urged people who got into difficulties with voting-machines to ask for help. On the screen the curtains of a voting-booth shook and a squeaky voice called 'Help!' Governor Rockefeller got 4 per cent of the Republican vote.

Governor Reagan could not point to the same handicaps. His name was on the Oregon ballot, as it had been in Wisconsin and Nebraska. His account of things was that he was to be nominated at the Miami Beach convention as a favourite-son candidate, simply to hold California Republicans together; so it was only honest to leave his name on the ballot in states which required an affidavit of complete non-candidacy if they were to take it off. A boyish frankness was part of his public face. So was a boyish modesty: right up to the first day at Miami Beach he maintained the pretence of not being a candidate in earnest. For that reason he stayed out of his three primary states during their primary campaigns. But with the approval of his national headquarters he was seen in them on television.

With very little television in Wisconsin he won 11 per cent of the Republican vote: in Nebraska, with scarcely more television, his score was 22 per cent. In Oregon the television investment was at least doubled. Oregon was a less conservative state than Nebraska, but it was nearer California. The Reagan share of the vote went up only one point, to 23 per cent. It was a chief reason why party professionals ceased to look on Governor Reagan as a prospect for the presidency until his brief blaze in the last two weeks before the Miami Beach convention.

All advertising has to address itself first to the weaknesses of the product. It is because of latent doubts in smokers about the virility and cleanliness of smoking cigarettes that tobacco advertisements show strong men enjoying them beside mountain streams. Ronald Reagan's weaknesses were that he had been an actor and that he had less than two years' experience in government. Nothing much could be done about the theatrical past except to play it down. In 1966, when he ran for the governorship of California, Reagan commercials deliberately eschewed show-business smoothness and glitter.[2] The tone was recaptured for 1968. In general the Governor behaved less like an actor than did, for example, Mr Lindsay, the *jeune premier* of the other wing of the Republican party: with his light, resonant voice and rising inflections the Mayor sometimes sounded in public like an understudy going on for Richard Burton at Stratford and determined to make the most of it. Shortness of service in government, on the other hand, could be turned into a positive asset. Ronald Reagan was the plain man in politics: the citizen who brought nothing with him into the halls of government except honesty and common sense.

So the chief Reagan propaganda instrument on television was a half-hour film made in Portland and San Francisco without benefit of east-coast expertise and entitled *Ronald Reagan, Citizen Governor*.

The first scene of the film was the occasion in January 1967 when Ronald Reagan was sworn in as governor of California in the rotunda of the state capitol at Sacramento. It happened just after midnight. The new governor made a joke about being on late-night television again, as his old films often were still, and launched into his inaugural address.

'Someone back in our history – I wasn't too good a student, but I think it was Benjamin Franklin – said: "If ever someone could take public office and bring to public office the teachings and the precepts of the Prince of Peace, he would revolutionise the world and men would be remembering him for a thousand years." I don't think anyone could ever take office and be so presumptuous as to believe he could do that, and follow those precepts completely. But I can tell you this: I'll try very hard.' At that point there was a barely perceptible break in the Governor's voice, and a pursing of his lips. Just visible in one corner of the screen was the mouth of the California supreme-court judge who had administered the oath. It quivered; and Mrs Reagan could be seen watching her husband with a wide, wet gaze.

(In her generation of the wives of western politicians Nancy Reagan was by far the most accomplished platform listener to her husband's speeches. Her parted lips and shining eyes were a paradigm of wifely attentiveness. Her nearest rival was Beryl Maudling, wife of the Conservative deputy leader in Britain. Both women had worked in the theatre: what they had brought away was not the counterfeit feeling but the discipline of the stage.)

The film continued with an ingenuous account of how Richard Nixon had been defeated for the same governorship by Pat Brown in 1962, and Pat Brown by Ronald Reagan in 1966. There were scenes of Ronald Reagan campaigning for Barry Goldwater, campaigning for himself, reporting in often-used phrases on the achievements of his administration: how they had saved money, for instance, by not throwing away official stationery which had Pat Brown's name on it. 'The girls just X out the other name and put mine in; and you know,' with a spreading smile, 'I get a certain amount of pleasure out of that.'

But the core of the film in its final version was a passage from a speech delivered to Republicans in northern California the month before the Oregon primary. It was a virulently written and professionally delivered attack on the recent Johnson record in Vietnam; and it laid Ronald Reagan bare as a man who could neither compromise nor forgive because he could not understand. 'One who abandoned, who abdicated the leadership will now treat with an enemy; and those in his party who would replace him whimper only that they would not have waited even this long to give the enemy across the table the victory that he couldn't win on the field of battle. And what of the young men, bleeding their lives into the rice-paddies and the jungle-trails of that faraway land? If their sacrifice was in vain, if it was not in our national interest for them to be there in the first place, who put them there, and why? And if it is in our national interest for them to be there, why is it suddenly no longer so? And why, why have they been denied the victory they are so capable of winning?'

The whole film was shown six times in Oregon, but this central passage was made into a five-minute item and shown repeatedly. Other parts of the film were similarly used: Benjamin Franklin and the Prince of Peace made a neat one-minute spot.

Of the specially produced advertisements, many were filmed testimonials. One was spoken by a girl student who said she was for Governor Reagan because she was concerned about law and order. Law and order was already a code phrase of many meanings, and she was clearly using it to mean the prevention of rape: she was standing in a wooded city park in Portland. The point was underlined by the young Portland public relations man who had produced the material and who screened it for me at his headquarters. 'That's for the dirty old man vote', he said.

But the results suggested that he had misread the interests of Oregon voters.

*

The other candidacy that suffered grave harm in Oregon was Robert Kennedy's. One of the numberless ironies of his death in Los Angeles a week later, on the night of his close win in the California primary, was that he had already virtually lost his chance of being elected president in 1968. Although the antagonisms he aroused in life were washed away in his death, they had been so strong that the delegates to the Democratic convention could only have agreed on him as their candidate for one reason: their belief that no Kennedy could lose an election. This faith had been borne out by Senator Kennedy's wins in the Indiana and Nebraska primaries, but it was made groundless when he lost to Senator McCarthy by six percentage points in Oregon; and the Kennedy victory in California by a smaller margin was not enough to recover the family reputation.

Like Ronald Reagan, Robert Kennedy suffered the more for his defeat in Oregon because of television. Afterwards some of his workers believed he should have bought more television time; but he had bought enough to make it hard for them to plead that he had not put forward his best face. He had spoken to the voters in conditions over which he had complete control, and with a regularity which brought even the most casual viewers within reach.

Yet television never did Robert Kennedy the service he needed. Throughout his four primaries, television was his chief campaign instrument. The question he had to meet was not so much about his views as about his character. There were as many people who thought it astonishing that he should be considered fit for the presidency as there were who thought it obvious. This was an argument which paid, partisan television should have been able to settle, or at any rate to influence. Even though television may not always present character and capacity accurately, it can at least be used to present them plausibly and coherently. Yet the division of opinion among the voters of the four primary states remained as fierce as in the country at large.

Robert Kennedy himself seemed aware of the problem. Like all the major candidates, he used advertising agencies for the drudgery of television politics: buying time-slots and seeing that there was enough material to fill them. He employed a New York agency, Papert Koenig Lois, in the three primaries he won, and a Portland agency in Oregon. But he also deliberately allowed two independent producers, both of first-class attainment, to work separately and to some extent in competition on making the main television material which should justify him to the voters; as if from their rival efforts some definitive statement might emerge. In the event neither produced a thesis that was wholly acceptable in itself, and no synthesis was made.

One of the two men was Charles Guggenheim, head of a Washington company which made documentary films. His work spanned Robert Kennedy's brief career as a candidate. He made the half-hour biography which was widely seen and admired during the senate campaign from New York in 1964: he was to make the memorial film which was shown to the 1968 Democratic convention in Chicago. The virtues he respected in Robert Kennedy were private ones: self-deprecation and an active sympathy for other people. He accepted a comparison between Robert and John F. Kennedy voiced by a man who knew them both: 'Jack cared about humanity: Bobby cares about humans.'

The chief source of illustration for these qualities was inevitably the Kennedy family. One Guggenheim contribution to the Indiana primary was a half-hour film called *Tea with the Kennedys*. It was in part a dialogue between the candidate, his wife, his mother and Colonel John Glenn, the astronaut. The dust was also blown off the 1964 biography. There was no time to take out the sequences that had been designed specially for New York. One of them dwelt at length on that part of Robert Kennedy's schooldays which had been spent in Bronxville, to combat the notion that he had no real link with the state. (A joke current during the 1964 campaign had him asking 'Where *are* the Bronx?') Another deployed newsreel film of the Israeli troops among whom he had lived as a war correspondent in 1948. The target had been the New York Jewish vote. But changes were made where they had political point. The film already covered Robert Kennedy's zeal as attorney-general on behalf of negroes. To this was now added his zeal in pursuit of criminals. Law enforcement was more in fashion in 1968.

With due musical annotation, the film also dwelt on his happy relations with his own children. It was not an unfair point. No one who was with him in a throng of small children, as I happened to be once in Indianapolis, could be unaware of the deep tenderness in his disposition. The place was a playground for children of all origins. The candidate listened to their accounts of what they did, and touched their hair and their faces, with an absorption that seemed genuinely to exclude the cameras that crowded round.

This side of Robert Kennedy's character, affectionate and concerned, was all that needed to be stressed when the purpose was purely elegiac. Mr Guggenheim's memorial film for the convention had in it some of the New York biography, with new words spoken by Richard Burton. It showed crowd scenes which spoke without words of the passionate devotion that Robert Kennedy could excite. It ended with the end of Senator Edward Kennedy's faultless eulogy to his brother in St Patrick's Cathedral in New York, overlaid with a picture of Robert Kennedy walking away alone towards the Pacific across a shining wet Oregon beach. It left a vast audience in tears.

But to love and be loved is not of itself a sufficient qualification to be president of the United States; as was perceived by the second ·man who made Kennedy television in 1968, Richard Goodwin. After a beginning in academic life, he had written speeches for President Kennedy and then for President Johnson. He worked for Senator McCarthy in New Hampshire and Wisconsin, and again after Senator Kennedy's death; but he was in the Kennedy column from Indiana through to California. During the Indiana campaign John Frankenheimer, a Hollywood director of repute, was brought in by Fred Papert of the New York agency to direct one of the studio discussions which were at that time the bread and butter of the Kennedy television effort. He and Richard Goodwin formed an alliance which became increasingly important in that effort; and it was Robert Kennedy's method not to define the relative standings of the new alliance and the Washington production company and the New York agency, but to wait and see which one of them produced the best work.

John Frankenheimer had no interest in making programmes of less than half an hour in length, although Fred Papert believed that shorter items would reach more voters for less money; and Richard Goodwin needed room to present his picture of Robert Kennedy as a man of enormous intellectual energy. So more and more Kennedy television became Goodwin-Frankenheimer half-hour programmes crammed with recitations of the candidate's ideas in his own voice, and illustrated with his exertions on the campaign trail.

They were not a success. The ideas were often good, and the pictures were often good, but they seldom matched. While the candidate and his wife were seen walking along a beach, his voice was heard talking about schools; and when the picture shifted to schoolchildren, the words were off on the problems of the old. It was split-minded stuff, and television needs to be single-minded. The best passages were the ones where the candidate said nothing at all. For the campaign he had revived the failing cause of American passenger rail travel: he rode the Wabash Cannonball through Indiana, and special trains through the Willamette valley in Oregon and San Joaquin valley in California. Colour television had point here. Watchers in summer clothes, holding balloons and babies, flashed past the windows of the train; and the sound-track was taken up with crowds cheering and a singer strumming the hobo ballad about the Cannonball: 'From the great Atlantic Ocean to the wide Pacific shore...' At those moments, sound and picture were in partnership: for the rest, they were distractingly in competition.

The fault, partly the product of haste, proved to be tactical as well as artistic. The thing that many Oregonians voted against in Robert Kennedy was what they called Eastern edge: they disliked the feeling that they were being overwhelmed by a young millionaire in a hurry, and from the other side of the country at that. It was exactly the flavour of the picture presented on television.

In the end the Goodwin-Frankenheimer account of Robert Kennedy's qualifications was no more persuasive than the Guggenheim account. Robert Kennedy was a difficult man to present as an intellectual force. He did not talk well. He seemed aware of it himself. It was painful to him to finish a paragraph: he was always left with the sense that his thought could be better put. So he talked on, and fast: too fast for lucidity.

American producers think two words a second a good rate for the commentary that accompanies documentary film. Broadcasters in Britain talk a little faster; but they usually regard three words a second as a decent maximum. At the start of an answer to Indiana students which was used as a commercial right through to California, Robert Kennedy spoke 172 words in 43 seconds, or four words a second; and his regular rate of delivery was over three and a half words a second. He talked like a man who knew that the time allowed to him was short.

During the primary campaigns, many of which had an effective length of a fortnight or less, these paid political interventions were by far the most noticeable because most abundant manifestation of television politics. But they were supported by a good deal of unpaid matter too: especially that stand-by of bush television, the panel interview show.

These interview programmes were one of Senator McCarthy's chief campaign weapons. 'You don't have to have anything to say to appear on television', he once said, in some surprise that anyone should think you did. But his gentle scorn did not extend automatically to people who worked in television. He addressed his questioners as if he were a friendly but very senior don conducting a seminar with students slightly stupider than the ones he was accustomed to teaching. Yet he was too polite even to imply in words that he thought them stupid. When he was asked to assent to some proposition he thought ill-based, he would begin his answer with 'Well, I don't really know.' It became a catch phrase. On a Sunday midday programme in San Francisco he used the phrase or a shorter version of it eleven times in barely twenty minutes. He had a don's dislike of expressions he thought threadbare, like 'counter-productive' or 'alarm and despondency'. His jokes were for the most part of the take-it-or-leave-it kind favoured by dons. There was only the smallest movement at the corners of his mouth when he once said of the North Vietnamese: 'They haven't tried to figure out American politics. It's understandable, I think, that they – that they wouldn't try: that they've decided that this is a hopeless proposition. We can't figure it out ourselves.'

He sometimes used the tutorial method in earnest. On CBS's *Face the Nation* two days before California voted he was asked why after twenty years in Congress his name was on no major legislation. 'Name me four people', he said, 'whose name is on major legislation.' His questioners, two CBS men and a columnist from the *Washington Post*, tried to let this go by; but he held them to it, demonstrating that it was necessary to go back into the last century to find four names. The original questioner put the point another way: Senator Kennedy had the reputation of being a creative, imaginative legislator.

'He has, ah?' said Senator McCarthy. 'What did he create or imagine, do you know?' No response except a surreptitious laugh from a sympathetic member of the panel who was out of shot. 'I think I've had a significant effect on the tax laws in this country. There are at least three or four things in the foreign aid bill of sixty-six... I think I'm a good legislator: I think I'm probably better informed in the broad legislative field than – than I think probably anybody in the Senate, if you want it straight.'

The exchange illustrated both the Senator's refusal to worship at the Kennedy shrine and his coolly self-evaluative confidence. The bad relations between Senator McCarthy and the Kennedys went back at least to July 1960, when the Senator had besought the Democratic convention with more fervour than realism not to reject Adlai Stevenson in favour of John F. Kennedy. Relations worsened in November 1967, when Robert Kennedy gave no support to Eugene McCarthy's declaration of candidacy against President Johnson, although the two senators shared the same view of the Vietnam war; and again in March 1968, when Robert Kennedy discovered in the McCarthy vote in New Hampshire a reason to stand for the presidency after all. Kennedy people thought it unsportsmanlike of Senator McCarthy not to congratulate their man on his wins in Indiana and Nebraska: Senator McCarthy thought it childish of Senator Kennedy to threaten to give up if he lost in California. This was the atmosphere which kept many Kennedy loyalists out of the McCarthy column after the murder in Los Angeles; and such rapprochement as there was in Chicago came too late.

Senator McCarthy had no doubt that the Oregon primary, the only one where he had defeated Senator Kennedy, had been the only one where the electorate had been able to make 'an objective and informed choice'; just as he had no doubt that the poor who had not voted for him in Indiana or California would vote for him once they knew him. His trust in himself was described as interior strength by those who loved him and as arrogance by those who did not. During a television interview on the educational network in July 1968 he said: 'If you challenge the king, you know, you have to be prepared for death, they say: if you challenge the president you have to be prepared to be president.' Despite all the claims that he would be a do-nothing president, he seemed to feel wholly prepared.

Out of this came his greatest strength on television: his unselfconsciousness. He was not exercised about the effect he was creating, because he felt sure that on right-thinking people the effect would be favourable. It was his greatest outward difference from politicians like Vice President Humphrey or Mr Nixon, who seemed at every moment of the day their own closest observers. It was the chief source of his attractiveness to the new generation, and the most promising sign of a new spirit in American politics: that there should be a presidential candidate more concerned with explaining his own thoughts than with manipulating other people's.

A side consequence of this comparatively effortless style was that the Senator remained in astonishingly good physical shape throughout the nine months of campaigning that led up to the Democratic convention in August 1968. They had been strenuous months: he played ice-hockey in New Hampshire (and, he said, 'pretty near died doing it – that was the most violent thing I've done in any campaign'); took a group of reporters, most of us at least fifteen years his junior, for a long jog round the back streets of Milwaukee; canoed on the Willamette river near Portland, and played catch at the San Francisco Dodgers' ballpark. His luggage regularly included baseball gear. But the chief indicator was the state of his throat. In the month before the conventions Mr Nixon was saving his strength, Vice President Humphrey was silenced by flu, and Governor Rockefeller was painfully hoarse. Senator McCarthy, after a longer spell on the road than any of them, was in full and untroubled voice. It was the reward of never having raised it.

His television advertisements betrayed the knowledge that some of the voters might think this odd. It was arranged that one of his interview appearances in San Francisco should be immediately followed by a 20-second McCarthy commercial which began: 'His manner is very quiet. But don't be misled. This man toppled a president.' While this was being said, the candidate could be seen cleaving his way through the flashbulbs. The form was typical of the McCarthy spot announcements. The voice went on: 'It took unusual strength to do what McCarthy did; and don't we desperately need that strength in the White House – now?'

The Senator himself gave off no air of desperation. He would have liked the job of president, but he was the one candidate of 1968 who seemed not to need it. He started out, in November 1967, with no belief that he could get it: the belief only came to him, and pleased him, when he surveyed his gleeful followers in a downstairs room at the Sheraton-Wayfarer Hotel in Bedford, New Hampshire, on the night of the primary result in March 1968. He had already lost the belief again when he went to Chicago in late August, and the loss gave him no pain. Insouciance and self-sufficiency are powerful virtues on television. On *Face the Nation* the day before the convention opened he made no attempt to dissemble his own knowledge that his campaign was a sinking ship. He said as much, in his last answer on the programme, when he explained why he could not leave his movement and become Mr Humphrey's vice-presidential candidate: 'It would be like the captain of the ship getting into the first lifeboat and saying "Well, fellows, there are enough lifeboats for everyone, but I'm going now."'

The freshness of the approach was emphasised a few minutes later when a rival candidate was being questioned on ABC's *Issues and Answers*. With his campaign in even worse shape, Senator George McGovern fell back on the kneejerk optimism of the regular politician.

Senator McCarthy's unwillingness to speak for effect was sometimes frustrating to his partisans, who were given no opportunity to demonstrate their devotion. But there were occasions, as during his last big speech of the California campaign, when he indulged his mystic sense of communion between the leader and the led. For a huge indoor crowd of his supporters at Santa Monica he had been reviewing what seemed to him the romance of his campaign. He talked of how neither the Kennedy nor the Humphrey faction seemed to expect to capture the other's forces; 'but both sides', he said, 'seem to say they want my people'. Above the cheers and laughter a voice could just be heard near the Senator's microphone saying 'Because we're the best, that's all.' Senator McCarthy took this up. 'You're the best', he said, with the upward inflection which often discouraged applause because it indicated that he had more to say: 'you're the ones that are most needed.'

From the back of the hall came a gruff shout of protest: '*You* are'; and it was taken up by other voices.

'All of us here', the Senator answered; and the audience released their affection and their hopes in nearly a minute of applause.

It was one of the most successful of his speeches; and it became also one of the notable television occasions of the year through the accident that the McCarthy people had put television outside-broadcast cameras into the hall, to make a videotape recording for subsequent use. The method enabled the television director to superimpose one picture on another; so that the crowd was seen through the head of their idol as he looked out over them. On his face there was a kind of love.

When he could be heard again he dissipated the mood with a joke about Henry the Fifth before the battle of Agincourt. It was an allusion he returned to. The lines beginning 'This day is called the feast of Crispian' were clearly in his mind when he said a few moments later: 'And I think that all of us who are here tonight, when ten years from now or twenty years from now – perhaps somewhat later than that for some of you – when asked what you did in nineteen hundred and sixty-eight, you'll be glad to say that you were here: that you were active'; and there, despite a double upward inflection, the applause broke in: 'that you did what you could. – And even if you're not asked I think some of you may well bring it up some time.'

Students of English literature in the audience, of whom there will have been a good many in such a hotbed of the higher learning as southern California, may have remembered that King Henry, after a similar joke – 'He'll remember *with advantages* What feats he did that day' – went on to use the phrase: 'We few, we happy few . . .' It was Vice President Humphrey who had laid claim, in his declaration of candidacy in Washington in April, to the politics of happiness. This was one of the few occasions when that ideal seemed to have been realised.

It was the last for many weeks. The speech was shown as a paid half-hour programme throughout California the night before polling. It displaced a workmanlike McCarthy biography. Barely twenty-four hours later Senator Kennedy was shot in the Ambassador Hotel in Los Angeles.

Just as funerals are the only events for which whole families gather, so they are the only events which whole nations watch. Out of a population of 200 million, 150 million are believed to have watched some part of Robert Kennedy's funeral observances in New York and Washington. For Martin Luther King's funeral in Atlanta two months before the audience had been almost as great. These were audiences which explained the faith of public men in television, and yet which never bestowed this degree of attention on any of them while they lived.

15 The Word Made Visible

It was Robert Kennedy's death, two months after Martin Luther King's, that roused Nelson Rockefeller. The two-month Rockefeller campaign then undertaken showed more understanding than any other of what television can do, and what it cannot, towards expounding a political message.

Until the murder in Los Angeles, Governor Rockefeller had vacillated. At the end of 1967 he was still saying that ambition was dead in him. His implied change of mind in February 1968 hastened Governor Romney's collapse and yet failed to take advantage of it. In March he said on live television that he was not a candidate. At the end of April, after Dr King's death and the disturbances that followed it, he said he was. Even then there was no fervour in his campaign. The preparations made were largely precautionary. Governor Rockefeller travelled, but not to Oregon, where he might have collected a useful vote in the May primary. He had won there in 1964 with the slogan: 'He cared enough to come.' Now he allowed a brief visit on his behalf by the Mayor of New York. The only harvest was a satiric newspaper advertisement which said: 'He cared enough to send Mayor John Lindsay – so write in John Lindsay for president.'

This strange trance was only broken when Robert Kennedy died at the beginning of June. Within a week Governor Rockefeller had renewed his candidacy with a rapidly assembled half-hour programme on networked television; and from then until his defeat at the Republican convention early in August his campaign was waged with a new and sustained intensity.

Dr King's death had in the Governor's opinion revealed reconciliation as the country's chief need. Senator Kennedy's death had not merely made the need more pressing, but had left no likely leader to meet it. Most people were already convinced that the next president would be either Mr Humphrey or Mr Nixon. Governor Rockefeller's defensible belief was that neither of them could do the job, and that he could. He had the expertise: he had the potential popular support.

All he did not have was the Republican delegates. Most of them already preferred Mr Nixon. The only strategy available to Governor Rockefeller was to try to show them through the opinion polls that he was more likely than Mr Nixon to be elected in November. Instead of offering inducements to the few, the Governor had to offer arguments to the many. It was an essay in the new politics because there was no time for the old politics.

Some traditional methods were used: a great deal more travelling, and a great deal of newspaper advertising. But the biggest and most expensive and most widely seen part of the effort was deployed on television.

The work was done by the agency that had handled Nelson Rockefeller's 1966 campaign for the New York governorship, Jack Tinker and Partners. The new advertisements were made after methodical consultation with the Governor's staff, and broadcast on over two thousand occasions: some nationally, most from stations in west coast and north-eastern states. There were no more than eighteen separate advertisements, each shown repeatedly: most of them lasting just under a minute, some just under five minutes. Seven of them were late-comers which reported the Governor's progress: eleven, the main ones, reported his policies.

This they could do in some detail when they had nearly five minutes to fill. One such piece simply showed the Governor reading to a mid-July press conference the four stages of his plan for peace in Vietnam. Not even the *New York Times* had published it at such length. Another carried part of a speech in which he had explained why he thought it more economical for local needs to be met out of state than federal tax money.

There were five of those longer pieces. But it was the six original one-minute advertisements which represented the fine flower of respectable political persuasion on television. The words were spoken not unskilfully by the Governor himself, casually identifying himself part-way through, and the pictures were related to what he said. He was only seen, in still photographs, in the item which explained why he was a candidate. He appeared in none of the others. When he complained that in South Vietnam the United States had 'overwhelmed a small country' without providing security or a government, fragile charm was perfectly expressed in a sequence of film shots of the Saigon river-front with an accompaniment of temple bells.

The other four short items all used a single film shot. Fifty seconds is a long time to hold a single shot, particularly when it is the whole of the film. In one of them the scene opened on what appeared to be a still picture of a mean city street on a rainy evening. 'Three thousand black men', the Governor's voice began, 'were among those brave Americans who have died so far in Vietnam. One hundred thousand black men will come home from Vietnam. What will they make of America? These men, who risked their lives for the American dream, and come home to find the American slum – what will they make of the slums, where too often jobs are as rare as hope? This is Nelson Rockefeller; and I say they deserve more than this . . .' Only then did the viewer realise that it was not a still picture: that the sound of footsteps came from a figure now moving into the light of the street-lamp in the foreground. It was a Negro soldier with a kitbag on his shoulder. He stood and looked up at the darkened tenement. And all the while a woodwind obbligato recalled, with infinite melancholy and irony, the jaunty Civil War song which begins:

> When Johnny comes marching home again,
> Hurrah! Hurrah!
> We'll give him a hearty welcome then;
> Hurrah! Hurrah! . . .

When Governor Rockefeller talked about removing objections to the draft system which called men into the army, a draft card burned on the film. But the film was run backwards, so that a card almost consumed by flames at the beginning was whole again at the end. Then there was the diminishing dollar bill that stood for inflation. Another unbroken shot was taken from inside a gun shop, looking out of the window at people who came one by one to look in at the guns; and on the sound-track the Governor offered his prescription for city life, beginning: 'A century ago a man bought a gun to protect himself in the wilderness. Today he buys one to protect himself in the cities.'

The special virtue of these advertisements was that they recognised where television's bounds were set. The ideas dealt with were serious and important without being too difficult. (Inflation proved the least tractable: the fall in the value of money was made more graphic without being made more understandable.) The ideas were presented one at a time. They were so briefly handled that the viewer had no time to be bored. Each idea was also expressed at the same time in a picture that matched it exactly. The pictures were interesting enough to engage the attention; but because they then only developed, instead of changing, they were not so interesting as to tug the attention away from the words. Where the idea could be further supported by other sounds besides speech, other sounds were heard.

But eight weeks were not nearly long enough to let Nelson Rockefeller make the conclusive mark he needed on the opinion polls. That was his campaign's epitaph: there was very little wrong with it except that it began absurdly late.

All that year, no other candidate's word to the voters was so expertly made visible. In general it was not a television election. No special dexterity with television was shown by the three main candidates left in the struggle at the end, or by the men whom they employed. None of the three derived any advantage from television which was denied to the other two. Television shed some of the mystic importance it had taken on during the 1960 election. In 1968 it remained a central channel of information; but as a campaign instrument it began to take its place in the same category as other methods of political expression old and new – banners held up in crowds, or slogans printed on the hat-bands of plastic straw hats.

Television was marked off from these other methods chiefly by its expense. At the end of the campaign, even before any detailed figures had been established, it was clear that great sums had been laid out. In return for his broadcast spending of at least $8 million Mr Nixon became for a while as insistent an advertiser as some of the biggest firms in America. When he took a share during October in sponsoring ABC's television relays from the Mexico City Olympics, among his fellow advertisers were Coca-Cola, Schlitz and Ford. Mr Humphrey's managers spent less all told than Mr Nixon's, but more in the last week of the campaign.

Sums of this size could not be raised by organisations with too strict a regard for virtue or the law. Although business firms were forbidden by federal law from making political contributions, both sides took money from committees which had been set up under unrevealing names inside individual companies to funnel contributions from senior employees. The Democrats revived the President's Club, which sold vague promises of access to a Democratic president for $1000 each. Twenty national Republican committees were late in lodging even such simple declarations of expenditure as were required.

To that extent television exerted its old effect on campaign morality. Its effect on the course of the campaign was less marked.

It is true that the two pronouncements which had the weightiest impact of the campaign year were both made on television. They both came from President Johnson at the White House: his disclosure at the end of March that he was not after all a candidate, and his announcement at the end of October – five days before polling day – that he was to stop the bombing of North Vietnam. To consider only their domestic effects, the first turned a closed contest for the Democratic nomination into an open one: the second was the chief influence which in the end brought the Democratic candidate within half a million votes of the Republican. Yet it was clearly what was said, not how it was said, which gave these broadcasts their importance. President Johnson's words would have had exactly the same impact if they had been issued in written form to the wire services.

The President used television because it was there. The immense resources of the American networks had made it the chief because the most convenient means of national communication. It had taken on a semi-official status which was especially clear on election night. Television was in charge of the count. The three men who controlled the election coverage of the three networks were in effect the nation's returning officers. An official count would also be made in each of the state capitals; but the official certificate of the vote from several of the state governors would not reach the Administrator of General Services in Washington until after the electoral college had met in mid-December.

The figures broadcast on election night were supplied by the News Election Service – a pair of computers in New York fed from seven regional centres which collected telephoned results from some 125,000 people. (In fact the computers began coming to palpably implausible conclusions even before the polls had all closed, and were retired in favour of a slower system.) The News Election Service had been set up by the two wire services as well as the three networks; but it was the networks whose use of the information seemed to constitute official publication. On the morning after polling day the Associated Press and United Press International both ruled Mr Nixon the winner in Illinois, the state whose electoral college votes gave him the total he needed, a few minutes after eleven in the morning. But CBS had still not joined the other two networks in the same opinion. CBS finally agreed about Illinois at a quarter to twelve. Only then, at the Leamington Hotel in Minneapolis, did Mr Humphrey dispatch a telegram to Mr Nixon and come down to the fading rococo ballroom to concede defeat.

George Wallace, the third man of the election, owed very little of his transitory eminence to television. His chief campaign weapon was the oldest of all: the formal public speech. Of the three candidates he was by far the ablest platform orator. Even without Mona and Lisa, two seasoned Southern belles who warmed his audiences with renderings of 'In those old cotton fields back home' and 'Are you for Wallace?' (to the tune of 'Are you from Dixie?'), the itinerant Wallace rally would have been the most entertaining show on the road. The reaction of its patrons was the proof. Night after night they showed up the standing ovation for the perfunctory and embarrassed thing it was: they gave Mr Wallace jumping ovations. When he came to his famous denunciations of briefcase-totin' bureaucrats, or pointy-headed professors who couldn't park a bicycle straight, the shock of delight and recognition would bring thousands of people leaping to their feet, their arms stretched high above their heads, to begin clapping before their feet even touched the ground.

This power in Mr Wallace as a speaker was not well distilled on television. The most emotive passages in his speech – 'If any demonstrator ever lays down in front of my car, it'll be the last car he'll ever lay down in front of' – were seldom carried on news programmes: news crews had to look for what was fresh in the speech, not what was familiar. And although his southern-fried syntax was a part of Mr Wallace's rhetorical armoury, an establishing of kinship with plain folks, he seemed himself to feel that it needed tidying up when he spoke principally for television. 'The folks that lay in the streets – or lie in the streets, rather...', I heard him say when he announced his candidacy in February 1968 to a dozen film cameras in a small room at the Sheraton Park Hotel in Washington. Television bothered him.

It may have been partly the self-consciousness of class. He ought not to have felt inhibited by the fact that television brought in people of a higher educational level than commonly attended his rallies: as he rightly pointed out from the platform, 'There's more of us than there is of them.' But boyhood insecurities die hard. Or perhaps it was simply that Mr Wallace disliked television, as he disliked the newspapers, because it was a means of contact with the voters which he could not control. When he criticised journalists, television reporters did not escape: 'All they know,' he said, 'they got a sweet voice.' He could foresee with some accuracy when television evidence would be used against him. In Eutaw, Alabama, in June 1968 an ABC cameraman filmed him shaking hands with an imperial wizard of the Ku Klux Klan. The greeting might have been less kindly viewed in other parts of America. But there were advantages in being on home territory. All Mr Wallace's bodyguards were from the Alabama constabulary. With his approval, one of them pulled the camera from the cameraman's shoulder and tore the film out of the magazine.

When General Curtis Lemay was introduced in October as the American Independence Party's vice-presidential candidate at a press conference on live television from the Pittsburgh Hilton, Mr Wallace tugged at the General's jacket to stop him enlarging too joyously on the use of nuclear weapons. The gesture was a mistake: it too was transmitted.

Television contributed to Mr Wallace's decision not to hold a party convention. He knew he would attract more critical than uncritical notice. Yet even when he used television in conditions he could control, the results were for the most part stilted and unpersuasive. When he broadcast in paid time, his family were woodenly paraded before he settled down to deliver a softened version of his unvarying speech: it badly needed an audience, and the programme was too long at half an hour. When the speech was once videotaped at a rally in order to make a paid programme, Mr Wallace lost his touch with a crowd and the tape was unusable. His best half-hour show was a sequence of news-film excerpts from several different rallies; and even then the strongest lines were left out.

A great many small sums of money were sent to Box 1968 at Montgomery after these appearances. Television did not pull Mr Wallace down any more than it had lifted him up. There were those who maintained that what lowered his stock from 21 per cent in the late September opinion polls to little more than 13 per cent of the final popular vote in November was the voters' late discovery, which they might have made on television, that his manifesto was all negative and contained no remedies. He suffered much more from that familiar and fatal embrace, the two-party squeeze.

The other two main candidates were less wary of television: Mr Humphrey in particular. Yet it cannot be shown that television's effect on either his or Mr Nixon's campaign was more than neutral.

Mr Humphrey regularly said things which implied slight regard for television advertising as a campaign instrument. The people wanted to know their candidate – 'to look at him, feel him, touch him, smell him': Madison Avenue was not America; and so on. In fact Mr Humphrey used paid television as much as he could: his decrials of it were most frequent during the time when the stop-Bobby funds had been used up and the stop-Nixon funds were not yet coming in; and he revealed himself on television more freely than most candidates. Mr Nixon, on the other hand, unfailingly spoke well of American television and the commercial principle in it. A number of advertising men served on his personal staff during the campaign and went with him into the White House. If you dislike commercials, he said in September 1968 on a television interview in Denver, go to a country where there is government-controlled television without commercials – he mentioned no names – 'and you'll come back to the U.S. and say "Give us the commercials"'. Yet he approached television with extreme circumspection, and withheld any disclosure of character on television as deliberately as he did in other public appearances. Nearly all his most thoughtful speeches of the campaign – on what the presidency was for, on the alienation of Americans from their government, on new alliances in American politics, on black capitalism – were delivered not on television but on radio. They contained more reflection than Mr Nixon thought admissible before a television camera or a public meeting, and they got more notice in the newspapers than a written statement would have done. They also cost comparatively little in broadcast time and almost nothing in production.

One of the qualities which breathed from Mr Humphrey's appearances on interview programmes throughout the summer was that he was anxious to be liked, by his interviewers as much as by his president. Mr Nixon could live without that. If he flattered the journalists who appeared with him on television – by using their

Christian names, remembering what they had written, pretending to believe that newspapers which had employed them were dignified by the association – it was to win their good words, not their affection.

Mr Humphrey made his most important campaign speech on television: his declaration from the studios of KUTV Salt Lake City at the end of September that as president he would stop the bombing of North Vietnam, in certain conditions. It represented the smallest possible breaking of step with President Johnson, but it did at least halt Mr Humphrey's slow march to disaster. Even in that speech it was demonstrated that just as Shakespeare would sacrifice the most solemn effect for a pun, so Mr Humphrey would drop everything for a cliché. The speech had been endlessly written and rewritten: yet when the authorised version finally passed before his eyes on the teleprompter, and Mr Humphrey found himself promising in the final paragraphs to wage a vigorous, tireless and forthright campaign, he could not forbear adding: 'I shall talk to you from my heart and from my mind.' 'This nation', a sentence or two later, inevitably became 'this great nation'. It was a kind of tic.

On television as in other things Mr Humphrey was a true son of the Upper Mid-West, where to leave any feeling unexpressed is to be thought as cold as a Minnesota winter. The effect of this usage as a rule of life is to cheapen all feeling: particularly when it is seen on the small screen, where understatement is often sufficient statement. When Mr Humphrey came before the live television cameras at the Leamington Hotel at noon on the day after polling and said 'I have done my best: I have lost: Mr Nixon has won: the democratic process has worked its will', his admirable words were cruelly made less and not more moving by the fact that he had tears in his eyes and a catch in his voice. His watchers all over the country had no need of a nudge to help them imagine what he was feeling then.

Mr Nixon, a man of discipline if ever there was one, understood this point well enough. Half an hour later he appeared before the cameras at the Waldorf Astoria in New York. It was an astonishing peak in an astonishing life. The grocer's son from Yorba Linda had narrowly lost the presidency eight years before: now, after a descent into the pit in between, he had narrowly won it. What was Mr Nixon's reflection on achieving his personal grail after so many changes of fortune? 'I can say this,' vouchsafed the President-elect: 'winning's a lot more fun.'

Mr Humphrey cared less for his interior dignity than Mr Nixon did. CBS filmed both candidates as they waited for their own nominations in their convention hotel rooms in August. (The film itself had a Chinese-puzzle quality: the two men were seen on television watching television.) Mr Nixon, sharply conscious of the camera, said little during and after the roll-call of the states except that it was all according to form. Mr Humphrey bounced up and down throughout and finally touched his hand from his lips to the television screen when his wife appeared on it. On a New Jersey beach in September Mr Humphrey rolled his trousers up to the knee, provided the photographers with candidate-alone-by-the-sea pictures which were a pastiche of the ones taken of Robert Kennedy in Oregon, and lost a race with a reporter from *Time*. Mr Nixon's furthest departure from the norm in the presence of film cameras was to play 'Home on the range' and 'Let me call you sweetheart' on the piano. Late in the campaign, when it became a possibility that he would lose Texas – as he did – he added to his public repertoire 'The eyes of Texas are upon you'.

Mr Humphrey was beyond argument the more talkative of the two on television. Mr Nixon remained able to answer questions in an average time of two minutes. Mr Humphrey was in laconic form if he answered more than four questions in half an hour: his record, achieved when he was being interviewed by a panel of local dignitaries, was a thirteen-minute answer to the Mayor of Buffalo.

Both candidates made some of their worst mistakes of the campaign on television. Abetted by his advertising men, Mr Humphrey used a paid half-hour broadcast in mid-October to promise an 'offensive against crime': it was before he realised that he had lost the conservative vote anyway and would be better employed trying to salvage the moderate vote. The next day a coalition of Negro leaders, the National Committee of Inquiry, decided to withhold the endorsement they had been ready to give him.

Mr Nixon deepened his vice-president trouble on television. Governor Agnew had said a number of tactless things at the beginning of the campaign, but was fairly discreet thereafter, except that he was pressed by a television interviewer in Detroit into the assertion that 'when you've seen one slum you've seen them all'. In an editorial late in the campaign the *New York Times* renewed certain conflict-of-interest charges against Mr Agnew. The charges had been argued before, the *Times* is not very widely distributed outside metropolitan New York, and it would have been safe enough to let the issue go. But Mr Nixon, making his first appearance on a network interview show for almost two years, said on *Face the Nation* that the *Times* was engaging in 'the lowest kind of gutter politics'; and at once Mr Agnew's land and bank holdings in Maryland became a principal subject of talk throughout the country in the last week of the campaign.

The mistakes were not crucial. In the end most of the Negro vote went to Mr Humphrey by default, and Mr Agnew's presence on the Republican ticket did not consign it to defeat, even though he could not deliver his own state of Maryland.

It would be too much to say that Mr Humphrey told all on television; but he told more than Mr Nixon. Hence the pressure on Mr Nixon to agree to a television debate with Mr Humphrey. Many Democrats believed it would open the oyster. Mr Nixon held fast to a reluctance based on his 1960 experience and on the pointlessness of risking his lead, and no debate was held.

Mr Humphrey did his best to make Mr Nixon's avoidance of debate a central issue of the campaign. He never let a speech go by without mentioning it; particularly during the period when money was tight and a debate would have meant valuable free television time. Mr Nixon clung to the sanctity of the two-party system as a reason why debate would be impossible. When the relevant committee of the House of Representatives, still wrestling with the necessary change in the law, approved a formula for debate which would include Mr Wallace, Mr Nixon said he would not engage in a three-ring circus. The formula was approved by the whole House only after Mr Nixon's Republican friends had spun the sitting out into one of the longest on record. Republican obstruction in the Senate killed the measure altogether. Mr Humphrey nevertheless reserved an hour with CBS for a three-handed debate. Mr Wallace indicated that he would not take part unless Mr Nixon did, and it was made clear that Mr Nixon could not take part unless Mr Wallace did not. Mr Humphrey decided to use the hour for himself. He spent some of the time talking from a desk which had two empty desks beside it, and he had difficulty filling the rest. 'Mr Humphrey debated an empty chair', Mr Nixon happily told audiences from Michigan through to Pennsylvania, 'and lost.' Mr Humphrey's advertising men had three puppets built for a mock debate on election eve, and then abandoned the idea as 'rather childish'. Mr Wallace said he would tolerate a Nixon-Humphrey encounter which excluded him if he were allowed time to reply later. Mr Nixon's press secretary said this changed nothing: 'We're not going to do a thing that would give George Wallace free time.' Twelve days before polling, the issue was finally let drop.

It had undoubtedly embarrassed Mr Nixon, not least because of what he had himself written in the *Saturday Evening Post* to embarrass President Johnson in the campaign summer of 1964. 'I believe that television debates contribute significantly to four major objectives which are in the public interest: a bigger vote, better informed voters, lower campaign costs and, in the end, a better president.'[1] At the same time it was difficult not to have a certain sympathy with Mr Nixon now. Mr Humphrey's record in the matter was at least as inconsistent. As senate majority whip in 1964 Mr Humphrey had on his own admission helped arrange that President Johnson would not be troubled by a bill permitting debate. More recently, in April 1968, Mr Humphrey had declined a three-man meeting with Senator McCarthy and Senator Robert Kennedy; and again in August he had called off a debate with Senator McCarthy.

Further, the only value which Mr Humphrey could hope for from a debate was the negative one that Mr Nixon might make a bad mistake. It was unreasonable to suppose that a debate could elicit positive information on opinions or intentions. Mr Nixon had contrived to stay unspecific through nine months of campaigning: he could hardly be expected to be more frank in an hour of carefully regulated television courtesies.

The nearest thing to a confrontation between the two men was a pair of almost concurrent telethons on the night before polling. Both were transmitted from the Los Angeles area: Mr Humphrey's from an ABC studio in Hollywood, Mr Nixon's from an NBC studio in Burbank. Earlier in the day Mr Humphrey had proposed telephoning a question from his studio to Mr Nixon's.

Both candidates were on the air for four hours: two hours for the whole country except the west coast states, then an hour's break, then two hours for the west coast. Mr Humphrey had a half-hour start. During that first half-hour he competed with himself: a half-hour film about him was run on NBC. The same film had been shown an hour before on CBS. Viewers found Mr Humphrey a hard man to avoid that night.

Telethons have to go out live, so that viewers can telephone at the right time; but there are ways of minimising the risk that the candidate will be seen at grips with an offensive or time-wasting caller. The Nixon programme followed the formula that had worked well for him in the Oregon primary. Questions telephoned by viewers were taken down by a hundred uniformed switchboard girls: the written questions were then scrutinised by Nixon staff members and selectively forwarded to the urbane Bud Wilkinson, who was free to modify the wording and to add questions of his own. Mr Humphrey's callers were able to have their own voices heard on the air, and without any delaying device except a studio question-master who brought them up on his loudspeaker desk; but they had first to be passed as articulate and well-disposed by a telephone panel of about forty.

Many of these forty Humphrey telephonists were lights of show business, and they had to be heard no less than the callers from outside. So from time to time they paraphrased the questions they had been getting. In consequence two more Hollywood figures were on hand to smooth the transition between callers and telephonists; these two and Mr Humphrey had to pad round the studio carrying their microphones; and the cameras had to swing about like telescopes on a seaside promenade. All this created opportunities for untidiness and error which were fully taken. One Hollywood figure forgot what he was to say. The telephonists were not introduced at the outset and seldom properly pictured: the first clear intimation to viewers that Frank Sinatra was manning a telephone was when he was seen, in sudden close-up, refusing to accept a reverse-charge call. Kirk Douglas spent some time audibly wondering whether his microphone was live. The flashing light which advised the studio audience to applaud appeared in shot.

Another complication was the presence beside Mr Humphrey of his vice-presidential candidate, Senator Muskie. The Senator had been one of the successes of the Democratic campaign, for the reason – which ought not to have been remarkable – that he addressed the voters like an adult talking to adults. But the fifth-wheel character of the vice-presidential post is always most apparent when the deputy is seen with the chief; and beside his patron the Senator became simply another face to be included from time to time, another voice to be heard, another microphone lead to clutter the studio floor.

None of these distractions found their way into the Nixon studio a few miles away in Burbank. Governor Agnew was safely on the stump in Virginia, on the other side of the continent; and the whole Agnew affair was got out of the way at the beginning of each two-hour session, when Mr Nixon warmly defended him in answer to a prearranged question from Mr Wilkinson. Mr Nixon was the undisputed star of his own show. Tricia and Julie Nixon were discovered among the telephone girls and briefly interviewed, and Julie's fiancé David Eisenhower read a message from his grandfather which commended Mr Nixon's statesmanlike response to the Vietnam bombing halt. With those exceptions, Mr Nixon's unruffled and undetailed responses flowed steadily for four hours.

Mr Humphrey, in Hollywood, had his moments of encouragement. In the first quarter of an hour Senator McCarthy telephoned from New York to say that he hoped he had cleared the way for his friends to vote for Mr Humphrey: the Senator seemed to feel that his recent promise of a markedly unenthusiastic vote for the Democratic ticket had been a thought ungenerous. And Mr Humphrey got his few seconds of debate with the Burbank studio. It was reported to him that Mr Nixon had said the North Vietnamese were taking advantage of the bombing halt to resupply their troops. Mr Humphrey leant into the lens. 'There is no indication of increased infiltration, Mr Nixon', he declared. 'And let me say that it does not help the negotiations to falsely accuse anyone at this particular time.' Mr Nixon was even drawn to reply, though not directly: he later mentioned a UPI report that the Ho Chi Minh trail was clogged with trucks.

The two programmes might have been mounted as an allegory of the two parties and the two campaigns. On the one side sat Mr Nixon, well advised, well staffed, brooking very little participation from the rank and file, and giving a highly efficient performance: on the other Mr Humphrey, ill advised, ill staffed, overwhelmed with participation, and yet surviving it all in better shape than could have been expected.

Viewing figures for New York City indicated that, for the ninety minutes during which they ran together, Mr Humphrey had a larger share of the audience in the first half-hour and Mr Nixon thereafter; but that the film *La Dolce Vita*, a serial comedy called *Family Affair* and Carol Burnett's hour of revue all had greater drawing-power than either. A Sindlinger national survey suggested that throughout that day, the day before polling, nearly 87 million Americans watched or listened to political programmes. 69 million of them heard both main candidates, and about the same number had already decided how to vote anyway. But the other 18 million were still worth playing for.

There was little that was remarkable among the two candidates' other essays into paid television, though television advertisements were more fully reported in the newspapers than they had been before the conventions. Both the Nixon and the Humphrey campaign used a film biography of their candidate. The Democrats also had a film which admiringly recalled the last five Democratic presidents, together with scratched and jerky newsreel film of flappers doing the charleston to indicate the kind of thing that went on under Republican administrations. Both campaigns showed their candidate in session with groups of questioning citizens. Both used passages from those encounters as shorter advertisements. Both carved advertisements, too, out of the speeches in which their candidates had accepted nomination at the conventions. Both used testimonials from eminent citizens. Mr Humphrey leaned heavily on a few kind words from Senator Edward Kennedy, who read them as if he had not seen them before: the endorsement most often used on Mr Nixon's behalf was from Connie Francis, the singer.

A few passages from Mr Nixon's acceptance speech were re-recorded by the candidate with slightly different words and re-illustrated by his advertising agents, who were Fuller & Smith & Ross of New York. One was the passage where he invited his convention audience to listen to the voice of the forgotten Americans, the non-shouters, the non-demonstrators, who worked and saved and paid their taxes and cared. While Mr Nixon's voice was heard, still pictures caught dignified and even heroic moments in the lives of farmers or steel-erectors. It was a useful technique: moving pictures would have revealed them in the next frame as ordinary mortals. Another passage, from Mr Nixon's long peroration, pictured the faces of American children whose dreams were not matched by their waking lives.

There was a child in one of Mr Humphrey's advertisements: a child a few months old, wearing nothing except a nappy, being patted on the back as he lay against his mother's shoulder. The advertisement was brought out at the end of September, when Mr

Humphrey was still not sure where to lay hold of the law and order issue. 'I wonder what he'll be like when he's older', the mother could be heard musing. 'I hope he won't be afraid the way we are. There's so much violence now...' A little more of this, and a masculine voice came bustling onto the sound-track with Mr Humphrey's assurances: life would be safe with him; but for every jail Mr Nixon would build, Mr Humphrey would *also* build a house: for every policeman Mr Wallace would hire, Mr Humphrey would *also* hire a good teacher. And the baby sighed contentedly.

This attempt to have the problem both ways and come out for motherhood as well was the work of Tony Schwartz, who in 1964 had devised the Doyle Dane Bernbach commercial in which a small girl counting daisy-petals represented the world that Senator Goldwater might blow to bits. (Doyle Dane themselves had been dropped from the Humphrey campaign after the Chicago convention, and an *ad hoc* group of advertising men installed in Washington under Joseph Napolitan, a professional political consultant.) It was also one of the first advertisements of the campaign to pitch into any of the candidates by name. It was not the last. Another Schwartz commercial panned onto the words 'Agnew for Vice-President?' while a man laughed for about fifteen seconds on the sound-track; and his laughter only faded as the first caption gave way to a second, 'This would be funny if it weren't so serious...' It was Mr Schwartz's considered view that the best political commercials were the ones which gave least information, but 'organised the viewer's feelings'.

The attack on Governor Agnew was part of the justification claimed by the Republicans for the only advertisement of the campaign which gave serious offence. Without comment, it interspersed photographs of America's troubles with photographs of an insouciant Mr Humphrey. The beginning was mild enough, with pictures of a bearded young man shouting and Mr Humphrey making as if to speak. But then a positively gleeful Vice President was sandwiched between pictures of white American soldiers beleaguered in a Vietnam dugout and a small white boy peering out of a window in an American city slum. The only words were in the captions at the end: 'This time vote like your whole world depended on it' – 'Nixon'.

The Republicans only used the piece once. Numbers of people complained about it to NBC, the network which had screened it, or to newspapers; and the Democrats complained both to the network and to the Fair Campaign Practices Committee in Washington. It was one of the few complaints which the Committee had to deal with throughout the campaign. 'Unquestionably a cleaner campaign than sixty-four or sixty', said their director.

One of the neatest television political commercials of 1968 was broadcast on behalf of John Gilligan, who dispossessed Frank Lausche of the Democratic nomination for the Senate from Ohio. It related the difficulties of growing up in Ohio – schooling, traffic, air and water pollution – to the struggles of a small boy pulling a toy school bus, and a car, and a boat on a piece of string up a long flight of steps; which turned out, at the mention of new men in the right places, to be the steps of the United States Senate in Washington. The commercial was made by Charles Guggenheim.

But Mr Gilligan did not win the seat. He lost the November election to the Ohio attorney-general, William Saxbe.

What Mr Saxbe had instead was a song. The last quatrain gives the flavour well enough:

> William B. Saxbe
> Can see the right way:
> William B. Saxbe
> Is needed today.

Songs did much for television politics in the 1968 campaign. Some of them were used as singing commercials, and some as crowd rousers under the camera's eye; though the difficulty there was that the crowd seldom knew the words. When Senator McCarthy arrived at a rally of his supporters in the gymnasium of the University of Puget Sound during the Washington state Democratic convention in July, and the band struck up the 'Colonel Bogey' march, very few people there knew that they were supposed to be singing:

> Stand up: Eugene McCarthy's here:
> Stand up: stand up and give a cheer . . .

Wallace campaign workers got over this problem, and made a little money at the same time, by selling sheet music and records of the set songs. There was the George Wallace Waltz, for example, which ended:

He'll scatter the commies and pseudos like sheep;
So dance to the George Wallace Waltz, my sweet.

When the crowd could be persuaded to learn at least the chorus of a song, their singing greatly enlivened the television news coverage of a meeting; as I discovered in John F. Kennedy Square, Detroit, in mid-October, when Chubby Checker laboriously taught a small lunch-time crowd the refrain:

Give me that vote for Hubert Humphrey,
Give me that vote for Hubert Humphrey,
Give me that vote for Hubert Humphrey,
He's good for you and me.

Mr Checker would then sing the verse himself:

He has given us the Peace Corps,
And he wants an end to *all* war;
And he will do so much more
When he walks through the White House door.
So give me that vote . . .

The problem about musical electioneering, and part of the reason why it has not caught on in Britain, is that the home-made songs are of uneven quality and the good songs are in heavy demand. Another attempt to set the Humphrey campaign to music was made with a song from a 1967 Broadway musical, *How Now, Dow Jones*:

Will everyone here
Kindly step to the rear
And let a winner lead the way . . .

But the song became too popular to be distinctive. In 1968 it was used by at least a dozen candidates for governorships or congressional seats. Local bands along Mr Humphrey's way preferred to greet him with the University of Minnesota rouser, a football song which begins 'Minnesota, hats off to thee!' and descends rapidly into gibberish. 'Step to the rear' was much more often heard as a radio advertisement for the Lincoln-Mercury division of Ford cars.

Another advertising jingle became the nearest approach to a Nixon campaign theme. The tune to which Connie Francis sang a song called 'Nixon's the one' in her television advertisements was never whistled in the streets. But the slogan itself also fitted the tune of

'Take me along', which United Airlines had borrowed from a 1959 musical of that name to popularise husband-and-wife travel; and when Mr Nixon won the Republican nomination, his workers at the Miami Beach Hilton Plaza were glimpsed on television singing and even jiving to it.

Before 'Step to the rear', the top political song came from a 1960 musical called *Wildcat*. The Democratic candidate for the Senate in Indiana in 1962 found one version of it particularly useful, because it served as a guide to pronunciation:

> Hey, look him over
> He's your kind of guy:
> His first name is Birch,
> His last name is Bayh.

But when Senator Bayh successfully defended his seat in 1968, the song was not heard in Indiana. His Republican opponent had bought the rights. The Republican made no use of the song himself, but his anxiety that no unfair advantage should be taken of him was understandable. His name was William D. Ruckelshaus.

In sum, the 1968 post-convention campaign was accurately reflected on television as being an undistinguished one. Between February and August the American people had seen their president announce that he would soldier no more, and two of their most admired leaders murdered. They had seen George Romney's sudden fall, Eugene McCarthy's sudden rise, and Nelson Rockefeller's sudden changes of heart. They had seen two party conventions arrive by totally different routes at the same result: a candidate who excited nobody. Given all this, the autumn campaign could hardly help being anticlimactic. The electricity had gone out of it. As such the campaign was neither dignified by television nor much misrepresented by it.

PART VI

Conclusion

16 Observed Effects

There are broadly speaking two ways in which people who stand outside government can nevertheless influence its course. One is by choosing between leaders, and sometimes between courses of action, on election days. The other is by arriving at the kind of majority conclusion which becomes known as public opinion. The question which politicians want answered about television is what effect it has on these two forms of public decision.

The fear that television will in the end dictate electoral decisions is almost as old as television itself. It was recently expressed again by Robert MacNeil, the television reporter who moved from NBC to the BBC, in a book about American political television called *The People Machine*. 'Sooner or later, a major office is going to be filled by some computer-primed and wealthy nonentity put over by commercials as a national savior.'[1]

Should this happen, it would be fair to make the point that such a figure was not the first wealthy nonenity in politics. But the interesting thing is that it has not happened yet. So long after the beginning of the television age, no politician has yet been elected to high office chiefly because of television, in America or anywhere else. Further, the 1968 American presidential election gave striking proof that television makes a poor election agent. Candidates who could use it well themselves, like Ronald Reagan or Eugene McCarthy, did not in fact survive into the final stages. Candidates who had it well used on their behalf, like Nelson Rockefeller, fared no better. There were of course political forces working against these men: the fact remains that those forces were not neutralised by skill with television. Television could not upset the ordinary data of politics.

Further, the men who did come through in 1968 were remarkably little indebted to television for their success. Richard Nixon and Hubert Humphrey were both established in the American political system well before television was: they were both in the Senate by 1951. If Mr Nixon was helped by television at the time of his 1952

Checkers broadcast, he was hampered by it at the time of the 1960 debates. Neither he nor Mr Humphrey was ever considered any more persuasive on television than they were personally; and certainly they did nothing in 1968 to reverse that reputation. Not even their commercials showed any special flair.

George Wallace is an even clearer case. Neither his rise to the status of a national third-party candidate, nor his fall to very near the point where candidates in British parliamentary elections lose their deposits, was noticeably television-engineered. It had been an old dread among people mistrustful of television that a demagogue's simple and inflammatory appeal would one day have disproportionate effect because of television. It never happened to Mr Wallace. He used television uneasily and unfruitfully. His movement grew by methods that had been much longer in service: volunteer work and mass meetings. It shrank again not because of anything Mr Wallace said or did, but because the Democrats began to reclaim their natural supporters, particularly among factory workers in the North.

Clearly television has helped men into office. So have a great many other political and natural forces. The choice of leaders has always been to some extent accidental: the most that television has done is to reinforce the importance of some of the accidents. Good looks, and verbal dexterity, and wealth have always been useful to politicians: television has only made these qualities a little more useful. Television has not turned them into necessary conditions of success, still less sufficient conditions: Senator Charles Percy, with all three, remained the least favoured of all five main contenders for the 1968 Republican presidential nomination. And other accidents are still as important as they were. Consider the accident of birth, especially in America: even setting aside the Kennedy phenomenon, there is still a certain usefulness in being called Long in Louisiana, Byrd in Virginia, Symington in Missouri, Stevenson in Illinois, LaFollette in Wisconsin or Rockefeller practically anywhere. Or there is the accident which held Richard Nixon back in 1960 and pushed him forward in 1968 – the accident of finding oneself in the path of a general sentiment that it is time for a change. None of these chance selectors owe their existence to television, and none have disappeared because of it.

Many politicians are themselves not persuaded that television is the domesday election weapon. They use television in the spirit in which they use all other campaign aids: it is a millstone which cannot be left unturned. There were no claims at the end of the 1968 campaign that any contests had been won on television. (The exceptions were marginal and disputable: a widely shown film in the Democratic senate primary in Alaska, a debate in the senate election in Oregon.) If television were a potent electoral force, it might have been expected to do much towards breaking the old moulds of American politics. The new politics, the appeal to voters as individuals rather than as members of interest-blocs, ought to have benefited greatly from television, which enabled politicians to approach voters singly or in small groups. Since television showed the same scenes to the whole nation, it ought to have ended regional politics. Enforced alliances between people of differing interests and views ought to have been shown up as illogical. In fact the new politics took a beating, the principle of the regionally balanced presidential ticket was still honoured, and the old Democratic coalition almost held together under unprecedented stress. The case for regarding television as a dominant influence in electoral politics was no better made out in America in 1968 than it had been in the past.

There remains the question of television's power in forming and informing public opinion.

Here there could be a clear and crucial effect. The suggestion of this book is that public opinion is not wrongly informed by television, but inadequately informed. People who lean chiefly on television for reports of current events cannot always reach sensible judgments, because television's limited capacities only allow it to dispense limited information.

This is not the received view. The conventional wisdom about television is that it is a noble instrument misused: that if only the shackles of human greed and frivolity were struck from it, television would rank with the wheel and the printing-press as one of the great emancipators of mankind. Robert MacNeil, recognising 'serious shortcomings in electronic journalism', is in this tradition when he finds most of them caused by 'the subservience of the new journalism to the mass advertising-entertainment industry'.[2]

Advertising, no: even the work of broadcasting organisations which carry no advertising is not delivered from serious shortcomings. Entertainment, arguably: the damaging part of the conventional charge is that the new journalists themselves are a frivolous-minded lot.

This contention became a matter of public argument in Britain in October 1968 when two cabinet ministers who had both been concerned in the past with the Labour party's public appearance, Anthony Wedgwood Benn and Richard Crossman, made speeches critical of the way broadcast news was handled. Mr Benn summed up his points with the declaration that broadcasting was too important to be left to the broadcasters. It was only a crisper way of saying what he had been saying for years, that members of minority persuasions, and not just professional broadcasters, ought sometimes to be allowed to get on the air without editorial interference. But it was taken in many quarters to mean that broadcasting ought to be left to the government instead. The suspicion arose because the Prime Minister had recently renewed his disagreement with the BBC by publicly implying that they manipulated the news in his disfavour. In a television interview two evenings later Mr Wilson said his words had been meant as a joke; but the interview itself – his first formal television appearance for nearly a year – was given to ITV, and the impression of government animus against the BBC gave piquancy to his colleagues' later musings.

Mr Crossman, like Mr Benn, was more concerned with trivial-mindedness than bias in broadcasting journalists; though all three men would have agreed that the cure for both ills was for broadcasters to publish the opinions of politicians whole and without comment. Mr Crossman, in a Granada Guildhall lecture, almost gave the case away by acknowledging of television that 'one of the things it cannot do well is home political news'; but then he rallied to ask that there should be more political talks on television.

The term 'talk' was evolved by BBC radio in the thirties as a euphemism for lecture. Television can handle lectures; but television lectures, like university lectures, are less than pointful in the light of the invention of printing. True, Mr Crossman asked that these talks should normally be illustrated; but that only revives the original difficulty. If the illustrations are apt, the ideas they illustrate will not be very complex. If they are not apt, they are worse than useless.

In June and July of 1968 Governor Rockefeller's advertisements provided illustrated television lectures on his policies which could scarcely have been bettered. But his helpers could find no illustrations for his views on what should be done in Vietnam, or on the proper relation between state and federal finances. The Governor simply had to get on camera and read them; and before they could be fully understood they had to be heard several times.

The view that television is trivial, yet not incurably trivial, is an old one. In Britain it was adopted by the Pilkington committee on broadcasting in June 1962. 'Our own conclusion', they said as they made their report, 'is that triviality is a natural vice of television.'³ They spoke in the tone of a headmaster who observes that inattentiveness is a natural vice of schoolboys as he reaches sorrowfully for the cane. They quoted with approval the view that it was 'more dangerous to the soul than wickedness', and they believed that it should and could be corrected.

The committee were not speaking only of television news. If they had been, they could not have made the proposition defensible except by renouncing value-words like 'triviality' and 'vice' and abandoning the notion that these properties could be altered. When television reports current affairs it must operate within the scope allowed to it by the aptitudes of the human brain and the propensities of governments. As a reporter of politics, television is obliged by natural and artificial forces to focus on pictures more than ideas, the abnormal more than the normal, people more than issues, idiosyncrasy more than character, conflict more than synthesis, what rulers want to show more than what the ruled want to see. This has nothing to do with managerial avarice or journalistic myopia: these are the given facts.

The consequence is that when politicians and journalists do that part of their proper work which consists in setting out a situation in detail and offering specific suggestions for improving it, citizens who rely chiefly or wholly on television for their information are in danger of being left behind in the argument. There is by now not much serious argument left about whether it is a good thing to promote racial harmony, or rebuild slums, or keep down inflation, or avoid foreign military involvements. The argument is about how, not whether. It is about the how of these questions that people must vote. Yet television is not well equipped to help them with the how. Mass literacy has promised a slow advance towards an educated electorate which would have some hope of taking reasonably well-based decisions. That advance will not be sustained by an electorate which looks principally to television for its news.

This prospect becomes less menacing as soon as it is acknowledged. If television has gaps in its equipment, so have all other methods of reporting. Television assumes its proper place in the political system the moment voters at large realise that there is more to know than they can learn from television by itself.

Television's special strengths are matched by special weaknesses. Born late into the same world as newspapers and the radio, television is heir to different but equally numerous ills; and the viewer, no less than the reader or the listener, is right to treat the evidence of his senses with a due scepticism.

Notes

Chapter 1: The Limits of Vision

1 Newton N. Minow, *Equal Time* (New York: Atheneum, 1964), pp. 13–20, 48–55, 75–6
2 Fred W. Friendly, *Due to Circumstances Beyond Our Control . . .* (New York: Random House, 1967)
3 Alexander Pope, *The Rape of the Lock*, iii 118

Chapter 2: Picture-Dealers

1 Joseph T. Klapper, *The Effects of Mass Communication* (Glencoe, Illinois: Free Press, 1960), pp. 68–72, 106–9
2 *Report of the National Advisory Commission on Civil Disorders* (New York: Dutton, 1968), pp. 362–89

Chapter 3: Were You There?

1 David Kraslow and Stuart H. Loory, *The Secret Search for Peace in Vietnam* (New York: Random House, 1968), pp. 186–98
2 Laurence Thompson, *The Greatest Treason: The Untold Story of Munich* (New York: Morrow, 1968), p. 256
3 *First Report from the Select Committee on Broadcasting, etc., of Proceedings in the House of Commons* (HMSO, August 1966), pp. xxviii, 142–4
4 Martin Harrison, 'Television and Radio', in D. E. Butler and Anthony King, *The British General Election of 1964* (London: Macmillan, 1965), p. 170: same chapter in same work for 1966 (Macmillan, 1966), p. 130
5 A. J. P. Taylor, *English History 1914–1945* (London: Oxford University Press, 1965), pp. 282–3, 367, 387

Chapter 4: The Interfering Eye

1 Marshall McLuhan and Quentin Fiore, *The Medium is the Massage* (sic) (New York: Bantam Books, 1967), p. 22
2 Rowland Evans, 'TV in the Political Campaign' (symposium), *Television Quarterly*, V i (Winter 1966), p. 25
3 *Political Campaign Financing Proposals*, U.S. Senate Finance Committee Hearings (June 1967), p. 286

4 James Reston, *The Artillery of the Press* (New York: Harper and Row, 1967), p. 86
5 *Dimensions of Television* (Washington: National Association of Broadcasters, 1967), p. 8: British Broadcasting Corporation Annual Report 1967–8, p. 134
6 Theodore H. White, *The Making of the President 1964* (New York: Atheneum, 1965), pp. 165–71
7 *Riots, Civil and Criminal Disorders*, U.S. Senate Investigations Subcommittee Hearings (December 1967), pp. 962–3
8 *Report of the National Advisory Commission on Civil Disorders*, pp. 366–7
9 Anthony Howard and Richard West, *The Making of the Prime Minister* (London: Jonathan Cape, 1965), p. 195
10 Allan Nevins, *The Emergence of Lincoln: Douglas, Buchanan, and Party Chaos 1857–1859* (New York: Scribner's, 1950), pp. 374–99: Robert W. Johannsen, ed., *The Lincoln-Douglas Debates* (New York: Oxford University Press, 1965), pp. 75, 86, 162, 237, 245

Chapter 5: An Electronic Serjeant-at-Arms

1 *First Report from the Select Committee on Broadcasting, etc.*, of *Proceedings in the House of Commons*, appendix 25
2 ibid., appendices 23 and 24
3 Commons *Hansard*, vol. 736, col. 1665, 24 November 1966
4 U.S. Senate Investigations Subcommittee, *Rules of Procedure* (1967), rule 9
5 Commons *Hansard*, vol. 736, cols. 1605, 1702, 24 November 1966
6 Commons *Hansard*, vol. 713, cols. 1076, 1082, 28 May 1965
7 Commons *Hansard*, vol. 713, col. 1088, 28 May 1965
8 Guy de Montfort, *Welcome to Harmony!* (London: David Marlowe, 1962)
9 *Second Report by the Select Committee on Broadcasting the Proceedings of the House of Lords* (HMSO, June 1968), pars. 13, 16
10 *Report of the Broadcasting Committee, 1949* (HMSO, January 1951, reprinted 1962, Cmd. 8116), par. 264
11 Lord Windlesham, *Communication and Political Power* (London: Jonathan Cape, 1966), pp. 213–14, 218–19
12 Ronald Butt, *The Power of Parliament* (London: Constable, 1967), pp. 309, 437
13 ibid., p. 401
14 Asa Briggs, *The History of Broadcasting in the United Kingdom*: vol. II, *The Golden Age of Wireless* (London: Oxford University Press, 1965), p. 135

Chapter 6: Say a Few Words

1 Federal Communications Commission Annual Report 1967, pp. 29–30

2 Alfred Friendly, 'Letter from London', *Washington Post*, 4 February 1968: William D. Hartley, 'Uninhibited TV', *Wall Street Journal*, 19 March 1968

Chapter 7: Mighty Opposites

1 Adlai Stevenson, 'Plan for a Great Debate', *This Week Magazine*, 6 March 1960
2 Kenneth S. Davis, *The Politics of Honor: A Biography of Adlai E. Stevenson* (New York: Putnam, 1967), pp. 483–4: Elie Abel, *The Missile Crisis* (Philadelphia: Lippincott, 1966), p. 169
3 Theodore H. White, *The Making of the President 1960* (New York: Atheneum, 1961), p. 178
4 Theodore C. Sorensen, *Kennedy* (New York: Harper and Row, 1965), p. 156
5 for the Kennedy-Nixon debates, White, *The Making of the President 1960*, pp. 279–95: Sorensen, *Kennedy*, pp. 195–206, 213: Bernard Rubin, *Political Television* (Belmont, California: Wadsworth, 1967), pp. 43–68, where further references are also given
6 Minow, *Equal Time*, pp. 29–31
7 Rowland Evans and Robert Novak, *Lyndon Johnson: The Exercise of Power* (New York: New American Library, 1966), pp. 473–4: James W. Davis, *Springboard to the White House* (New York: Crowell, 1967), p. 242n.
8 Howard and West, *The Making of the Prime Minister*, p. 156
9 Henry Steele Commager, 'Washington would have Lost a Television Debate', *New York Times Magazine*, 30 October 1960; reprinted in Commager, *Freedom and Order* (New York: Braziller, 1966)
10 Elihu Katz and Jacob J. Feldman, 'The Debates in the Light of Research: A Survey of Surveys', in Sidney Kraus, ed., *The Great Debates* (Bloomington: Indiana University Press, 1962), p. 203
11 J. G. Blumler and Denis McQuail, *Television in Politics: Its Uses and Influence* (London: Faber, 1968), pp. 100–5: cf. Joseph Trenaman and Denis McQuail, *Television and the Political Image* (London: Methuen, 1961), pp. 115–16, 122

Chapter 8: The Way to Downing Street

1 for the two incidents, Howard and West, *The Making of the Prime Minister*, pp. 26–7, 107–9
2 George Brown, 'Why the DEA lost to the Treasury Knights', *Sunday Times*, 31 March 1968
3 William Rees-Mogg, 'The right moment to change', *Sunday Times*, 18 July 1965
4 Howard and West, *The Making of the Prime Minister*, pp. 216–19
5 Butler and King, *The British General Election of 1964*, p. 162n., where full figures are given

6 'The 1964 General Election on Television: A BBC Audience Research Report', in Richard Rose, ed., *Studies in British Politics* (London: Macmillan, 1966), p. 197
7 Hugh Noyes, 'Mr Heath tough with TV inquisitors', *The Times*, 17 October 1967
8 quoted more fully in Butler and King, *The British General Election of 1966*, p. 123
9 Taylor, *English History 1914–1945*, p. 436n.

Chapter 9: Television Studio to White House

1 quoted from the *Wheeling Intelligencer* in Richard H. Rovere, *Senator Joe McCarthy* (New York: Harcourt Brace, 1959), p. 125
2 Roy Cohn, 'Believe me, this is the truth about the Army-McCarthy hearings. Honest', *Esquire*, February 1968
3 Michael Straight, *Trial by Television* (Boston: Beacon Press, 1954), pp. 247–53
4 *Dimensions of Television*, p. 8: FCC Annual Report 1967, p. 161
5 *Dimensions of Television*, p. 8: White, *The Making of the President 1960*, pp. 293–4 and appendix A
6 Earl Mazo and Stephen Hess, *Nixon: A Political Portrait* (New York: Harper and Row, 1968), pp. 91–125
7 Eric F. Goldman, *The Crucial Decade – and After: America 1945–1960* (New York: Vintage Books, 1961), pp. 191–9
8 William V. Shannon, *The Heir Apparent: Robert Kennedy and the Struggle for Power* (New York: Macmillan, 1967), pp. 55–7
9 Gene Wyckoff, *The Image Candidates* (New York: Macmillan, 1968), pp. 50–1, 145–58
10 Tom Wicker, 'TV in the Political Campaign' (symposium), *Television Quarterly*, V i (Winter 1966), p. 16
11 quoted more fully in White, *The Making of the President 1964*, pp. 215–17
12 Stephen Hess and David S. Broder, *The Republican Establishment* (New York: Harper and Row, 1967), pp. 252–4
13 Kurt Lang and Gladys Engel Lang, *Politics and Television* (Chicago: Quadrangle Books, 1968), p. 30
14 Raymond R. Coffey, 'Police clubs shred image: Daley the big "casualty" ', *Chicago Daily News*, 29 August 1968
15 BBC Licence and Agreement (HMSO, December 1963, Cmnd. 2236), section 13: Television Act, 1964, schedule 2, section 8
16 David Karp, 'A Look Back Into the Tube', *New York Times Magazine*, 19 November 1967
17 Mrs Lyndon Johnson in an interview with Henry Brandon, *Sunday Times*, 20 August 1967
18 Communications Act, 1934, amended 1952, section 315b
19 Herbert E. Alexander, *Financing the 1964 Election* (Princeton: Citizens' Research Foundation, 1966), table 7

20 FCC, *Survey of Political Broadcasting, Primary and General Election Campaigns of 1964* (July 1965), table 1
21 FCC *Survey 1966* (June 1967), table 3
22 *Political Campaign Financing Proposals*, p. 380
23 title 18, United States Code, 1958 edn., section 610
24 *Political Campaign Financing Proposals*, p. 178
25 William Stafford, 'Connections', *Rescued Year* (New York: Harper and Row, 1966)

Chapter 10: Electoral Television and the Law

1 Federal Corrupt Practices Act, 1925; later title 2, United States Code, 1958 edn., sections 241–8
2 *Political Campaign Financing Proposals*, p. 184
3 Hatch Political Activities Act, 1939, amended 1940; later title 18, United States Code, 1958 edn., sections 608–9
4 State of New York, 1967 Election Law, section 455
5 Representation of the People Act, 1949, section 64
6 RPA 1949, sections 140, 146
7 Trenaman and McQuail, *Television and the Political Image*, p. 72
8 *Projections – Predictions of Election Results and Political Broadcasting*, U.S. Senate Communications Subcommittee Hearings (July 1967), p. 343
9 FCC public notice, 'Use of Broadcast Facilities by Candidates for Public Office' (April 1966), pp. 6662–9
10 BBC *Handbook* 1968, p. 153: Television Act, 1964, section 3 (2)
11 Communications Act, 1934, amended 1967, section 396 (f) (3)
12 FCC *Survey 1964*, table 7: 1966, table 5
13 RPA 1949, section 53 (2)
14 ibid., schedule 2, rule 45 (2)
15 *Conference on Electoral Law, Final Report* (HMSO, February 1968, Cmnd. 3550), annex B, section 33

Chapter 11: Velvet Glove

1 Communications Act, 1934, section 326
2 FCC, *Report on Public Service Responsibility of Broadcast Licensees* (1946)
3 '15 congressmen in broadcasting', *Broadcasting*, 15 January 1968
4 Drew Pearson and Jack Anderson, *The Case Against Congress* (New York: Simon and Schuster, 1968), pp. 176–8
5 ibid., pp. 163–75
6 FCC public notice, 'Applicability of the Fairness Doctrine in the Handling of Controversial Issues of Public Importance' (July 1964): FCC Rules and Regulations, vol. III, section 73.123: Communications Act, 1934, section 315
7 FCC, 'Editorialising by Broadcast Licensees' (13 FCC 12456, 1949)

8   Television Act, 1964, sections 18; 5 (3); 3 (1)
9   BBC Licence and Agreement, clauses 14 (3, 4); 20 (1); 24 (1): BBC Charter (H.M.S.O, June 1964, Cmnd. 2385), article 6 (3) (b)
10 *Report of the Broadcasting Committee, 1949*, par. 27
11 Harman Grisewood, *One Thing at a Time* (London: Hutchinson, 1968), p. 199
12 BBC Annual Report 1965–66, p. 41: 1966–67, p. 35
13 BBC Licence and Agreement, clause 14 (5)
14 *Broadcasting* (H.M.S.O, December 1966, Cmnd. 3169), par. 48
15 Barbara Wootton, *In a World I Never Made* (London: George Allen and Unwin, 1967), p. 262
16 *Report of the Broadcasting Committee, 1949*, par. 556

Chapter 12: The Voluntary Principle

1   'Appointment of Lord Hill "a bombshell" to BBC', *The Times*, 10 February 1968

Chapter 13: Watch and Vote

1   *Projections – Predictions of Election Results and Political Broadcasting*, pp. 163–5, 168, 211–19, 238–50, 250–66, 315–29, 360–3
2   Klapper, *The Effects of Mass Communication*, pp. 15 sqq., where several studies are summarised
3   Lang and Lang, *Politics and Television*, pp. 222–3
4   V. O. Key, Jr., *Public Opinion and American Democracy* (New York: Knopf, 1967), p. 396; and chapters 14 and 15 in general
5   BBC Audience Research, 1964, in Rose, ed., *Studies in British Politics*, p. 197
6   FCC, *Survey* 1960, table 42; 1964, table 18a; 1966, table 3
7   *Presidential Campaign Broadcasting Act*, U.S. Senate Communications Subcommittee Hearings (May 1960), p. 6
8   Herbert M. Baus and William B. Ross, *Politics Battle Plan* (New York: Macmillan, 1968), pp. 332–3
9   script reprinted in full in Windlesham, *Communication and Political Power*, appendix B
10 agreement published as appendix H in January 1951 printing of *Report of the Broadcasting Committee, 1949*
11 BBC Audience Research, 1964, in Rose, ed., *Studies in British Politics*, pp. 192–3: 1966, unpublished
12 Richard Rose, *Influencing Voters: A Study of Campaign Rationality* (New York: St Martin's, 1967), pp. 204–5
13 Key, *Public Opinion and American Democracy*, p. 346
14 Trenaman and McQuail, *Television and the Political Image*, pp. 187–93
15 Rubin, *Political Television*, pp. 3–4

Chapter *14: Screening the Candidates, 1968*

1 White, *The Making of the President 1960*, pp. 110–12
2 Bill Boyarsky, *The Rise of Ronald Reagan* (New York: Random House, 1968), p. 138

Chapter *15: The Word Made Visible*

1 Richard M. Nixon, 'LBJ should debate on TV', *Saturday Evening Post*, 27 June 1964

Chapter *16: Observed Effects*

1 Robert MacNeil, *The People Machine* (New York: Harper and Row, 1968), p. 327
2 ibid., p. 329
3 *Report of the Committee on Broadcasting, 1960* (HMSO, June 1962, Cmnd. 1753), par. 102.

Index

(names which appear only in the notes are not included)